Travel Guide to Croatia 2023

Your in-depth travel guide that will enable you to competently experience Croatia's attractions in 2023.

Timothy S. Balderas

All rights reserved. No part of this publication may be reproduced, distributed, or transmitted in any form or by any means, including photocopying, recording, or other electronic or mechanical methods, without the prior written permission of the publisher, except in the case of brief quotations embodied in critical reviews and certain other noncommercial uses permitted by copyright law.

Copyright © Timothy S. Balderas, 2023.

TABLE OF CONTENT

Introduction
Weather and climate of Croatia
Why visit croatia ?
The Best time to visit Croatia
Getting to Croatia
Getting around Croatia
Visas and currency

Chapter 1 : Must-see destinations
DUBROVNIK
SPLIT
PLITVICE LAKES NATIONAL PARK
HVAR ISLAND
KORCULA ISLAND
ZADAR
ZAGREB
PULA
ROVINJ
SIBENIK

Chapter 2: Things to do
Swimming and sunbathing
Hiking and Biking
Sailing and windsurfing
Visiting historical sites
Sampling the local cuisine

Attending festivals and Events

Chapter 3 : Where to stay
Hotels
Apartments
Hostels
Camping

Chapter 4: Where to eat
Restaurant
Taverns
Pizzerias
Bars
It
Chapter 5: Budgeting
Transportation
Accommodation
Food
Activities

Chapter 6: Tips for travelers
Frequently asked Questions
Conclusion

Introduction

Greetings from the enchanted country of Croatia! Southeast European country Croatia is well known for its breathtaking landscapes, rich history, and vibrant culture. This gem of the Adriatic offers visitors a range of captivating experiences, from ancient walled cities to charming beach towns.

Croatia's diverse geographic features provide an inviting backdrop for exploration. Given the more than a thousand islands that are sprinkled throughout its stunning coastline, it is no wonder that Croatia is recognized for its lovely beaches and crystal-clear oceans. Each area offers a special combination of local character, natural beauty, and history, from the well-known tourist hotspots of Dubrovnik and Split to the lesser-known island paradises of Hvar and Korula.

In addition to the beauty of its coastline, Croatia boasts eight spectacular national parks where visitors may immerse themselves in pristine nature. The unusual beauty of Plitvice Lakes National Park, a UNESCO World Heritage site, is comprised of a sequence of cascading lakes and waterfalls. Krka National Park is popular with tourists because of its beautiful swimming spots and ethereal waterfalls. For those looking for adventure, the wild mountains of Paklenica National Park and the enigmatic woods of Risnjak National Park provide wonderful hiking trails and animal encounters.

Croatia's natural beauty is complemented by a vibrant tapestry of history and culture. The country's historic towns are a true treasure mine of spectacular structures and fascinating stories. The Old Town of Dubrovnik, often known as the "Pearl of the Adriatic," is a UNESCO World Heritage Site that has imposing medieval defenses, opulent palaces, and meandering cobblestone streets. The palace of the Roman emperor Diocletian in Split is a living reflection of the past with its ancient ruins mingled in with modern shops and restaurants. Zagreb, a vibrant city in Croatia, blends opulent Austro-Hungarian architecture with contemporary cultural attractions including museums, galleries, and a thriving café scene.

Croatian cuisine is a delectable fusion of flavors from Central Europe and the Mediterranean. Take advantage of the fresh fish that has been caught nearby, traditional dishes like "Peka" and "Pljeskavica," or delectable treats like Pag cheese and Dalmatian prosciutto. Try rakija, a fiery spirit, or a bottle of local wine to go with your dinner for a complete understanding of Croatia's culinary heritage.

Croatia celebrates its rich cultural past by holding a number of festivals and events throughout the year. From the vibrant atmosphere of the Dubrovnik Summer Festival to the rich traditions of the Sinjska Alka knights' tournament, there is always something to see and do. Thanks to the varied assortment of trendy pubs, clubs, and live music venues that make up the nightlife culture in cities like Zagreb, Split, and Zadar, visitors can feel the vibrant spirit of the country after dark.

There are hotel alternatives in Croatia to suit every preference and budget. Whether you like lavish resorts, charming boutique hotels, or cozy guesthouses, you may choose from a range of options that provide comfort and friendliness. Your trip will also be remembered for the wonderful friendliness of the locals, who enjoy in touring visitors about their beautiful country and instructing them in its traditions.

As you go on your Croatian vacation, make this trip book your trustworthy travel companion. It will provide you information, counsel, and recommendations so that you may make the most of your trip. If you want to relax on stunning beaches, immerse yourself in history and culture, or explore the wonders of nature, Croatia has it all. Pack your bags and get ready to create everlasting memories in this amazing setting. Welcome to Croatia, a great and stunning nation.

Weather and climate of Croatia

Southeast European nation Croatia has a complex and diverse climate that is influenced by both its geographic setting and proximity to the Adriatic Sea. The country has a climate that is more Mediterranean at the coast and more continental inland. This uncommon mixture results in various climatic conditions and unique weather patterns during the course of the year.

Along Croatia's gorgeous coastline, the Mediterranean climate, which is characterized by hot, dry summers and mild, wet winters, is prevalent. From June through September, there is abundant sunshine in the coastal districts, and the average temperature ranges from 25°C to 30°C (77°F to 86°F). The Adriatic Sea plays a key role in controlling the coastline temperature by providing a refreshing wind throughout the hot summer months. These elements make the coastal regions suitable for beachgoers and sunbathers, including well-known tourist sites like Dubrovnik, Split, and Zadar.

The warm winters along the coast have an average daily temperature of between 5°C and 10°C (41°F and 50°F). However, it rains a lot this time of year in the coastal areas. Heavy downpours that come and go and intermittent thunderstorms are common. The wettest months are usually November and December, and as springtime approaches, precipitation gradually declines.

Croatia's interior has a more continental climate due to its proximity to the Dinaric Alps and the absence of the Adriatic Sea's moderating effect. Summers in the interior may be dry and sweltering, with regular highs of 30 °C (86 °F).

On the other side, winters may be harsh and frigid, with lows below freezing. As a result of the extensive wintertime snowfall, particularly at higher elevations, interior locations like Zagreb and Plitvice Lakes National Park are desirable travel destinations for those who like winter sports.

The spring and the autumn are the transitional seasons in Croatia. Throughout the spring (March to May), the temperature rises gradually, and nature comes to life with vivid foliage and lovely blossoms. Autumn (September through November) is characterized by cooler temperatures, especially inside, as well as breath-taking displays of fall foliage.

Croatia's climate is typically well-defined, however there may be regional variations due to differences in topography, elevation, and distance from the coast. The core mountainous regions have cooler temperatures and more precipitation than lowland locations. The islands that dot the Croatian coast also each have their own distinct microclimate because of their distinctive physical characteristics.

Additionally, Croatia has a lot of sunlight—2,600 hours on average each year. The amount of sunshine in this country contributes to its appeal as a tourism destination, especially in the summer when visitors throng to its beautiful beaches and islands.

Croatia has lately seen the consequences of climate change, much like many other regions of the world. Changes in precipitation patterns, an increase in the frequency of severe weather, and rising sea levels, which might have an effect on ecosystems and coastal populations, are some examples of this. To adapt to and decrease the effects of climate change, a range of measures are being implemented, including the use of renewable energy sources and sustainable tourism practices.

In conclusion, Croatia's weather and climate provide a vast variety of scenarios around the country. From the sunny Mediterranean coast to the chilly interior highlands, Croatia has a lot to offer year-round. Whether you're seeking for scorching summer beach days or freezing winter adventures, Croatia's environment provides a stunning backdrop for seeing its natural beauty and significant cultural.

Why visit croatia ?

Croatia, a captivating country located on the gorgeous Adriatic coast, should be on everyone's bucket list. Croatia offers a unique experience that will leave you wanting to return often due to its stunning natural beauty, rich history, vibrant culture, and kind hospitality. Here are a few convincing reasons for why visitors really must visit Croatia.

The coastline of Croatia is home to some of the most beautiful beaches in all of Europe. The metropolitan beaches of Split and Dubrovnik, as well as the lovely islands of Hvar and Bra, provide the perfect setting for relaxation and refreshment. These beaches also have crystal-clear turquoise waters. Whether you're searching for a peaceful getaway or an exciting beach party, Croatia's diverse coastline can satisfy all tastes and inclinations.

In addition to its beaches, Croatia is known for its breathtaking natural beauty. The country is home to eight great national parks, each with its distinct character. Plitvice Lakes National Park, a UNESCO World Heritage site, has lush forests, turquoise lakes, and cascading waterfalls that give the region a fairytale-like atmosphere. The Krka National Park offers swimming in emerald-green pools and admiring lovely waterfalls. The natural splendor of Croatia provides various opportunities for outdoor recreation, including anything from kayaking and sailing to hiking and biking.

In addition to its natural beauty, Croatia has a rich historical and cultural heritage. Dubrovnik, a lovely city known as the "Pearl of the Adriatic," is a UNESCO World Heritage site and is renowned for its stunning Baroque structures, ancient defenses, and picturesque Old Town. Split, a historic city, offers a glimpse into the Roman Empire with its renowned Diocletian's Palace, a still-standing monument of the past. In the historic city of Zadar, one may discover a remarkable blend of Roman ruins, medieval churches, and modern artwork, providing a unique cultural experience.

The dynamic cuisine scene in Croatia is a fantastic reason to visit. Enjoy a delectable variety of seafood delights, such as succulent lobster, fresh fish, and oysters. The country's many regional cuisines, which are influenced by Mediterranean, Italian, and Eastern European tastes, provide a wonderful gastronomic journey. If you serve your meal with one of Croatia's world-class wines produced in its stunning vineyards, you'll experience the perfect combination of flavors.

The welcoming nature of the Croatian people also adds to the allure of the nation. Croatians are known for their wonderful hospitality and like sharing their customs, legends, and rituals with visitors. Croatia will make you feel at home whether you're exploring a bustling market, taking part in a local festival, or just striking up a conversation with a friendly local.

Another reason why tourists like Croatia is because it is easily accessible and has a sophisticated tourism infrastructure. Due to the extensive network of airport and boat connections, getting across the country is straightforward and easy. The country offers a wide range of housing options, from luxurious resorts to cozy guesthouses and apartments, to accommodate all preferences and budgets.

In conclusion, Croatia is a seductive vacation spot because of its unique blend of unsurpassed natural beauty, fascinating history, vibrant culture, mouthwatering cuisine, and hospitable locals. If you want to relax on stunning beaches, travel through breathtaking national parks, take in the history and culture, or indulge in wonderful cuisine, Croatia has it all. You will undoubtedly have fond recollections of your visit to this endearing country and a wish to go again.

The Best time to visit Croatia

Croatia offers a variety of sights and a Mediterranean setting to appeal to all types of tourists. Even while Croatia may be visited all year round, certain seasons are regarded as the best for enjoying all the country has to offer.

In Croatia, the summer months of June through August are often the busiest. Bright, sunny days characterize these months, making them ideal for visiting coastal towns and the beach. Swimming and other water sports are best when the Adriatic Sea is at its warmest. The crowds are a disadvantage of this popularity. Well-known places like Dubrovnik and Split may have more tourists and higher hotel and activity fees. If you plan to travel during this period, it is recommended that you make reservations long in advance and be ready for more crowds.

The shoulder seasons of spring (April to May) and fall (September to October), which provide a more relaxing and economical experience, are the best times to visit Croatia. Despite the cooler temperatures and fewer tourists, the weather is still pleasant throughout these months. You could appreciate seeing the historical sites, national parks, and charming towns without the throngs of people. For travelers on a restricted budget, it is an appealing choice since housing and transportation expenses are often less costly.

Due to the abundance of blooming plants in the terrain, spring in Croatia is particularly beautiful. Cycling, hiking, and visiting parks like Plitvice Lakes and Krka are all enjoyable outdoor activities when the weather is nice. You may take your time strolling around the little streets, visiting the markets, and sampling the local cuisine at the beach towns since there are less people there.

Warm weather and a vivid display of foliage throughout the fall give Croatia its own distinct appeal. The coastal towns and islands become more intimate as the throng diminish. Wine enthusiasts may take advantage of the time to go to vineyards and attend festivals in locales like Istria and Peljeac. Without the throngs during the peak season, you may still go swimming and enjoy the peace and quiet of the beaches.

It's important to keep in mind that there can be intermittent rains throughout the spring and autumn. However, as they often provide a lovely mood, you shouldn't allow the rare showers prevent you from appreciating the country's natural beauty.

If you're interested in local events and traditions, you may want to plan your vacation around festivals and celebrations. The Split Summer Festival, the Zagreb Advent, and the Dubrovnik Summer Festival are just a few of the annual events that take place in Croatia. Visitors get a unique and comprehensive look at Croatia's rich cultural heritage via these activities, which include music, dance, theater, and visual arts.

In conclusion, the best time to go to Croatia depends depend on your priorities and tastes. If you like crowded settings, a wild nightlife, and beaches, the summer months of June through August are ideal. On the other hand, if you prefer a more relaxed and affordable vacation with lovely weather and less people, the shoulder seasons of spring and autumn are the best options. Whether you want to relax on gorgeous beaches, visit historic cities, or get lost in the natural beauty of national parks, you can always count on having a fantastic time in Croatia.

Getting to Croatia

If you are unsure about how to begin your enchanting adventure, let's look at the many ways you might travel to Croatia.

For overseas travelers, air travel is often the most convenient and efficient mode of transportation. Croatia is well connected to important cities across the world thanks to a number of international airports serving as the country's entrance points. The busiest airport in Zagreb, the country's capital, is Zagreb Airport. It offers a wide range of flights to cities throughout Europe and beyond. In particular for visitors visiting the southern shoreline areas, Split Airport and Dubrovnik Airport are two more popular entry points.

After arriving in Croatia, there are numerous methods to continue your journey. To get to Zagreb, the nation's capital, you may utilize the efficient public transit system. Buses and trams make it simple to go throughout the city, making it possible for you to learn about its fascinating history and culture. Due to its advantageous location, Zagreb is a great base from which to see the rest of Croatia.

Consider crossing the water to Croatia if you want a more picturesque approach. The country features a beautiful coastline that is dotted with idyllic islands and little coastal towns. From surrounding countries like Italy, Greece, and Montenegro, you may travel by boat to Croatia and arrive while admiring the breathtaking Adriatic Sea views. Access to several islands and coastal places is made possible by the ferry terminals located in the port cities of Split and Dubrovnik.

Taking the train to Croatia is an exciting option for anyone seeking a taste of Europe. The country is connected to its neighbors and has strong rail accessibility. You may combine several sites on your schedule thanks to the international train network's connections to cities like Vienna, Budapest, and Belgrade. When traveling to Croatia by train, you may completely enjoy the appealing surroundings because of the peaceful and attractive voyage.

Instead, road trips are a great opportunity to see Croatia at your own pace. The country has a decent road network, which makes driving around easy. If you're traveling from a close country like Slovenia, Italy, or Hungary, you may travel at your own pace through beautiful landscapes and charming cities. You may rent a vehicle from a variety of locations, providing you the opportunity to see both well-known tourist destinations and undiscovered gems.

When you get to Croatia, there are many of things to do. The stunning Plitvice Lakes National Park and the historic city of Dubrovnik with its majestic medieval walls are just two of the many attractions in Croatia that may satisfy the tastes of every tourist.

Whether you travel to Croatia by air, sea, train, or road, your unforgettable experience doesn't end when you arrive. Prepare to be mesmerized by the country's stunning natural beauty, immersed in its rich history, savoring its delectable cuisine, and experiencing the warm hospitality of its people. Croatia is where you are encouraged to go on an adventure that will provide you with memorable memories.

Getting around Croatia

Getting about Croatia is generally easy and pleasant thanks to a well-developed transportation infrastructure and a wide range of accessible modes of transportation. Whether you want to see the dynamic capital city of Zagreb, the picturesque countryside, or the charming coastal towns, there are a variety of options to suit your interests and travel needs.

One of the most common ways to see Croatia is by bus, thanks to its extensive network. Buses are a stable and cost-effective mode of transportation that connect the country's major cities, towns, and tourist destinations. Businesses like Croatia Bus and FlixBus provide dependable routes and pleasant services, making it simple to go between different regions. The majority of buses have air conditioning, are well-kept, and provide lovely views as they drive.

If you're looking for a speedier and more efficient option, Croatia has a robust rail network. The nation's rail business, Croatian Railways, operates trains that link important cities such Zagreb, Split, Rijeka, Zadar, and Dubrovnik. Train travel is a fantastic way to relax and enjoy the environment, especially while passing through gorgeous countryside. Researching the routes and schedules in advance is a good idea since it's crucial to bear in mind that certain remote regions may not be accessible by train.

For anybody interested in seeing the stunning Croatian islands, ferries are the ideal alternative. Croatia provides a distinctive and amazing experience with its broad coastline and more than a thousand islands. Frequent voyages are made by the main ferry operator, Jadrolinija, to popular destinations including Hvar, Brac, Korcula, and Vis. In addition to being a mode of transportation, these boats provide an opportunity to enjoy the beautiful waters and take in the refreshing sea breeze.

Renting a car is another excellent method to go about Croatia, especially if you want more freedom and flexibility. In large cities and airports, there are several car rental agencies that provide a selection of vehicles to suit various needs and preferences. You may go by yourself in a car to remote national parks, off-the-beaten-path destinations, and hidden gems. Nevertheless, keep in mind that parking might be challenging in crowded areas, so it's better to make enough planning.

In cities like Zagreb, Split, and Dubrovnik, public transit systems like trams and buses make it simple to move about. These networks provide access to well-known attractions, significant historical sites, and centers of culture. Additionally, for shorter trips or while carrying a lot of luggage, taxis and ride-sharing services like Uber provide a more direct and practical means of transportation.

Croatia is a cycling-friendly country with several bicycle routes and bike-friendly cities. Renting a bike is a terrific way to explore smaller towns, coastal areas, and stunning landscapes. Many travel agencies and rental firms provide bicycles, and some hotels even offer them as a complimentary addition to their guests.

To sum up, Croatia offers a multitude of transportation options, making getting around simple. Whether you choose for buses, trains, ferries, autos, or bicycles, you may successfully visit the country and take in its rich cultural heritage, gorgeous beaches, and breathtaking natural beauty. Thanks to its well-connected transportation infrastructure, Croatia ensures that going from one point to another is not only easy but also an enjoyable part of your whole trip.

Visas and currency

Before planning a trip to Croatia, travelers must get familiar with the country's visa requirements and currency information. It is possible to guarantee a pleasant and trouble-free travel by being aware of these elements. This page will include the visa requirements as well as information on the local currency.

To learn the specific visa requirements for travelers from non-EU countries, please visit the official website of the Croatian Ministry of Foreign Affairs or get in touch with the Croatian embassy or consulate nearest you. Many times, those who need visas have to apply for them before leaving. Normal requirements for the visa application process include a completed application form, passport photos, documentation of lodging, a trip itinerary, travel insurance, proof of sufficient funds, and a passport with a specified amount of remaining validity.

The official currency of Croatia is the Croatian Kuna (HRK). When visiting Croatia, it is advised to carry some local currency with you for convenience. Exchanging money is rather easy since there are so many exchange offices, banks, and ATMs available around the country.

The majority of hotels, restaurants, and shops accept credit and debit cards from other countries. However, it's wise to always have some cash on hand, especially when visiting smaller shops, local markets, or distant regions where there may not be many card payment options.

The Euro (EUR) is not the official reserve currency of Croatia since it is not a member of the Eurozone. While certain tourist-oriented businesses may accept Euros, it is often encouraged to use local currency since the exchange rates for Euros may not be as favorable. It is advised to compare rates at many locations in order to get the best deal possible when exchanging money. Additionally, keep an eye out for any unfavourable prices or hidden fees.

To avoid potential scams or overcharging for security reasons, it is essential to use care while handling cash and monitor exchange rates. It's also a good idea to let your bank or credit card provider know about your travel plans to ensure smooth transactions and prevent any unanticipated card issues.

Understanding the Croatian visa requirements based on your nationality and the purpose of your travel is crucial, to sum up. Being familiar with the local currency and knowing where to convert money will help make for a smoother journey. By keeping these factors in mind and making early planning, tourists may thoroughly enjoy their time seeing Croatia's beautiful landscapes, historic sites, and vibrant culture.

Chapter 1 : Must-see destinations

DUBROVNIK

Dubrovnik, on the southern coast of Croatia, is a must-see destination because it expertly mixes historic allure with spectacular natural beauty. This lovely city, known as the "Pearl of the Adriatic," is renowned for its stunning architecture, intact medieval defenses, and seductive cultural past. Visitors come here from all around the world. Dubrovnik is a fantastic place to visit since it offers visitors a fully immersive experience. Its lengthy history began in the seventh century.

One of Dubrovnik's most notable features is its imposing city walls. The Old Town is surrounded by these magnificent fortifications for two kilometers, which provide breathtaking views of the terracotta rooftops below and the azure Adriatic Sea. Walking around the walls is a must-do activity that enables visitors to go back in time and see the city's unique architecture from a different perspective.

Walking into the heart of the Old Town is like entering a real-life museum. The charming pedestrian lanes are adorned with elegant palaces, gorgeous churches, and squares with limestone pavement. The city's main boulevard, The Stradun, is bustling with activity and has a wide variety of cafes, shops, and restaurants. Examples of Dubrovnik's outstanding architectural beauty include the majestic Rector's Palace, the Franciscan Monastery, and the well identifiable Sponza Palace.

Dubrovnik is home to several historical and cultural sites that help to illustrate the city's extensive history. A visit to the Dubrovnik Cathedral, with its Baroque-style facade and Treasury housing the remains of the city's patron saint, is essential for both history buffs and art enthusiasts. A sizable collection of artwork, including pieces made by local artisans, is kept in the Dominican Monastery, which was founded in the 13th century. The nearby museums, including the Dubrovnik Maritime Museum and the Dubrovnik Natural History Museum, add to the background information on the region's history.

Along with its architectural wonders, Dubrovnik is home to breathtaking natural beauty. With its crystal-clear waters, the Adriatic Sea's hidden coves and gorgeous beaches beckon tourists. From Banje Beach, which is just a few feet from the Old Town, to the far-flung Lokrum Island, there are several locations to soak up the sun and chill down in the ocean.

Anyone seeking sweeping vistas must take a cable car ride to Mount Sr. The trek offers stunning views of Dubrovnik's terracotta-roofed houses, the endless Adriatic Sea, and the nearby islands. Tourists may enter the Imperial Fortress, a 19th-century fortress that now houses a museum on the Croatian War of Independence.

There's little doubt that Dubrovnik's culinary scene is a highlight of each visit. The city's proximity to the ocean makes fresh fish readily available, and local eateries expertly prepare it. From authentic Dalmatian fare to international specialties, Dubrovnik offers a broad range of dining options to satiate every desire.

To sum up, Dubrovnik is a mesmerizing place that expertly combines historical allure, great architecture, and natural beauty. Whether they wish to explore the ancient city walls, immerse themselves in the rich cultural past, or just relax on the stunning beaches, every visitor to Dubrovnik may find something to pique their interest. This jewel of the Adriatic, which is without a doubt one of Croatia's top tourist destinations, will leave visitors with long-lasting memories of its beauty and allure.

SPLIT

Split, a stunning city on Croatia's Adriatic coast, is a well-liked destination for travelers from all over the world. With its extensive history, stunning architecture, vibrant culture, and exceptional natural beauty, Split offers visitors of all interests a unique and memorable experience. Whether you like history, pursuing adventure, or just resting, Split has a lot to offer.

One of Split's biggest attractions is the Diocletian's Palace, a UNESCO World Heritage Site. This enormous building, which was built in the fourth century AD, is a marvel of architecture and illustrates the fascinating history of the city. Explore the place's winding alleyways, historic ruins, and breathtaking underground chambers. The palace is now a swarm of activity that pulls visitors in and transports them to a different era with its bustling markets, lovely cafés, and fascinating street performers.

In addition to the palace, Split is the location of numerous historical sites that will fascinate visitors who are interested in the past. Romanesque architecture is well shown at the Cathedral of St. Domnius. It was first built as Diocletian, the Roman emperor,'s tomb. Climb the bell tower for expansive views of the city and the Adriatic Sea. Concerts and other cultural events often take place in the Peristyle, which is the palace's main square. It provides a unique blending of traditional and contemporary experiences.

For those seeking natural beauty, Split has a stunning coastline with beautiful beaches and clear waters. The renowned swimming and sunbathing spot of Bacvice Beach is just a short walk from the city's core. Learn about the nearby Marjan Hill, a pine-covered natural area where you can go hiking, riding, or simply relax with a peaceful picnic while taking in the stunning views of the city and the sea.

Split's vibrant cultural scene is just another reason why it should be on everyone's agenda. All throughout the year, the city hosts a plethora of events that celebrate everything from wine and food to music and cinema. The Split Summer Festival features a range of theatrical and musical performances in magnificent outdoor venues, including the historic amphitheater. To truly appreciate the culture, savor authentic Dalmatian cuisine in the city's exquisite restaurants and regional wines in the lively wine bars.

Split serves as a gateway to the beautiful Dalmatian islands Hvar, Brac, and Vis. Take a boat to these wonderful islands to take advantage of their charming villages, seclusion, and crystal-clear waters. Each island offers a peaceful retreat from Split's hectic daily life and appeals in its own particular way.

Split has excellent public transportation, a world-class airport, and easy access. The city offers a range of housing options, from luxurious hotels to affordable hostels, to suit any traveler's preferences and price range.

In conclusion, Split has earned a reputation as a popular travel destination for good reason. Due to its exceptional blend of historical significance, natural beauty, vibrant culture, and proximity to the lovely Dalmatian islands, it is an inevitable choice. Whether you want to explore the ancient ruins of the Diocletian's Palace, relax on the stunning beaches, or learn more about the local way of life, Split is likely to leave a lasting impression and deliver unforgettable experiences for visitors.

PLITVICE LAKES NATIONAL PARK

In the middle of Croatia, the Plitvice Lakes National Park is a spectacular natural wonder that astounds visitors. With its cascading waterfalls, immaculate lakes, and lush vegetation, it's no wonder that this wonderful place has become a must-visit for travelers from all over the world.

The more than 295 square kilometer Plitvice Lakes National Park is Croatia's oldest and largest national park. Its diversified landscape is defined by a network of interconnected lakes and waterfalls that provide a fascinating network of turquoise-colored pools and flowing streams. The park's unique ecological value and exceptional natural beauty were recognized by being named a UNESCO World Heritage Site.

The Plitvice Lakes National Park's main attraction is its network of sixteen interconnected lakes, which are arranged in cascades and connected by a series of waterfalls. These lakes are renowned for their stunning colors, which vary from vibrant blue to deep emerald green, which are caused by the minerals and organisms that dwell in the water. The park's wooden boardwalks and pathways provide visitors breathtaking views of the lakes and waterfalls at every turn.

One of the park's most recognized attractions, the Veliki Slap, also known as the Great Waterfall, rises to a height of 78 meters. It is Croatia's largest waterfall and a stunning sight to watch as water tumbles over the moss-covered rocks into the pool below. The air is filled with a lovely mist, and the sound of the river flowing adds to the atmosphere.

Exploring Plitvice Lakes National Park is like stepping into a fantastical universe. The park is a refuge for individuals who like the outdoors and being in nature since it provides a variety of hiking trails that wind through the forest, across wooden bridges, and along lakeshores. The routes are well-maintained and fluctuate in complexity, making them accessible to both casual walkers and experienced hikers.

As visitors go across the park, they may encounter a variety of wildlife and plant species. Since the park is home to several bird species as well as bears, wolves, and lynx, it is a haven for birdwatchers and wildlife enthusiasts. The lush vegetation includes beech, fir, and spruce trees, creating a rich and diverse environment that is a delight to explore.

Along with its natural beauty, Plitvice Lakes National Park also offers amenities to enhance the visitor experience. There are cafes and restaurants located inside the park where visitors may relax and enjoy traditional Croatian cuisine while taking in the surroundings. Boat and electric train services are available for park visitors who want to go to remote areas of the park and see it from different perspectives.

Whether you visit Plitvice Lakes National Park in the spring to appreciate the vibrant colors, the summer to enjoy the lush greenery, or the autumn to take in the golden tones, each season offers a memorable experience. Each season, with its own unique beauty, transforms the park into a lovely sanctuary.

In conclusion, people may go to Plitvice Lakes National Park to find peace and natural beauty. Everyone who arrives is left with a positive image of the area by its gorgeous lakes, waterfalls, and surrounding woodlands. Whether you are a nature lover, an explorer, or simply someone who appreciates the beauty of the natural world, Plitvice Lakes National Park will capture your heart and soul.

HVAR ISLAND

Hvar Island, which is located in the Adriatic Sea off the coast of Croatia, is a stunning destination that attracts travelers from all over the globe. Hvar Island's magnificent natural beauty, extensive cultural heritage, and vibrant nightlife have made it a must-visit destination. Whether you're searching for leisure, adventure, or a taste of history, this enchanting island offers a range of activities that will leave you in awe.

One of Hvar Island's most alluring features is its breathtaking beauty. As you approach the island, a breathtaking landscape with tranquil coves, clear waters, and lush green hills welcomes you. The island enjoys a Mediterranean climate with long, sunny days and mild winters, making it a year-round tourist destination. On the island's coastline, visitors may discover quiet beaches like Dubovica and Zavala where they can unwind and soak up the sun.

In addition to its stunning natural beauty, Hvar Island is also rich in culture and history. The town of Hvar, which is located on the western coast, has a long and ancient history. Wander through the meandering alleyways studded with charming buildings from the Venetian era, see the Franciscan Monastery and its exceptional collection of artwork and artifacts, and admire the magnificent Hvar Fortress from the 16th century. The island is also home to a variety of attractive towns, each with its own unique charm and personality, such as Stari Grad, Croatia's oldest town, and Vrboska, often known as "Little Venice" because to its picturesque canals.

Adventure seekers may choose from a wide range of outdoor activities on Hvar Island. The island's diversified landscape is perfect for trekking and cycling, with trails that pass through wineries, lavender fields, and olive groves. The crystal-clear waters around the island provide several opportunities for sailing, swimming, snorkeling, and diving.

KORCULA ISLAND

In the turquoise waters of the Adriatic Sea, Croatia's Dalmatian archipelago includes the lovely island of Korula. Due to its fascinating history, breathtaking environment, and vibrant culture, this enchanting island is a must-see destination for travellers seeking both natural beauty and cultural immersion.

The magnificent environment of Korula Island first captures tourists' attention. When you arrive by ferry or boat, the island's historic city walls rise from the shore like a fortress out of a fable, adorned with cottages with orange roofs. While stunning beaches and hidden coves draw sun-seeking tourists, the mountains are covered with vineyards and olive groves. The island's diverse landscape, which has deep forests and verdant valleys, offers several opportunities for unhurried exploration.

The island's name-bearing town of Korula serves as a tangible reminder of its illustrious history. This ancient walled city, known for having been the residence of legendary explorer Marco Polo, is attractive in every aspect. As you look for hidden squares and lively cafés, explore the old stone houses that flank the narrow, cobblestone alleyways. The Gothic and Renaissance architectural wonders like St. Mark's Cathedral and the Bishop's Palace are a testament to the island's vibrant cultural history.

The unique traditions and mythology of Korula will captivate culture vultures. The Moreska Sword Dance, a centuries-old spectacle, captivates audiences with its intricate dance and cheerful music while reenacting a struggle between the Red King and the Black King. The several museums on the island, including the Marco Polo Museum and the Icon Museum, provide further details about its interesting past.

Wine connoisseurs may experience some of Croatia's greatest vintages on Korula Island. Native grape varieties thrive on the island's fertile soils and in the temperate Mediterranean climate, producing wines of the highest caliber. Enjoy the robust reds and crisp whites that have earned Korula its reputation as a refuge for wine lovers by seeing family-run vineyards, taking a wine tour, and visiting family-run vineyards.

Nature enthusiasts might find refuge on the island in its unspoiled beauty. Explore the beautiful woods of the Vela Luka region, where hiking trails meander through centuries-old olive groves and fragrant pine forests. Visit Lumbarda and Racisce, two stunning sandy beaches ideal for water sports, sunning, and swimming. The island offers wonderful opportunities for snorkeling and diving, allowing visitors to experience a wide range of marine animals and unexplored underwater tunnels.

On the island of Korula, the food is exquisite. Try the island's traditional dishes, which are influenced by flavors from the Mediterranean and the Adriatic, while enjoying the fresh catch of the day at charming beach eateries. Not to be missed are the powerful lamb and goat dishes prepared in ancient peka ovens, as well as the well-known Korula swordfish, which is served with local herbs and olive oil.

No matter what kind of traveler they are—those seeking relaxation, adventure, or cultural exploration—they will have a fantastic time on Korula Island. It is a location you just must see due of its stunning environment, intriguing history, and kind people. As the sun sets over the Adriatic and casts a golden glow on the ancient city walls, you'll understand why Korula Island has captured travelers' hearts for ages. Visit this Croatian hideaway and let Korula's timeless appeal to enchant you.

ZADAR

For travelers seeking the perfect balance of history, pristine environment, and vibrant modernity, Zadar, which is situated on Croatia's stunning Adriatic coast, is a must-visit destination. With its rich cultural past, breathtaking environment, and unique attractions, Zadar offers visitors from all over the globe an unforgettable experience.

One of the most well-known attractions in the city is its old town, a labyrinth of ancient streets and squares decorated with centuries-old buildings. By meandering through the narrow cobblestone streets, tourists may fully immerse themselves in the city's fascinating history. The Roman Forum, an archaeological treasure from the first century, showcases the remnants of ancient temples, basilicas, and columns, transporting visitors to the time of the Roman Empire.

Despite the fact that Zadar's history is undoubtedly intriguing, the city cherishes modernism. The Sea Organ, a creative architectural marvel, is a must-see site. When waves crash on the steps, hidden pipes under the surface provide a symphony of entrancingly beautiful sounds. The amazing moment travelers had while taking in the gorgeous sunset from the nearby solar-powered light show Greeting to the Sun will always be etched in their memories.

Another beauty that lures visitors to Zadar is its coastline. With its beautiful beaches and crystal-clear oceans, it offers a haven for relaxation and regeneration. The most well-known place is Nin, a charming town near to Zadar. The Church of the Holy Cross, the smallest church in the world, and the well-known Queen's Beach, noted for its therapeutic mud, are both located there. Swimming, tanning, and exploring the surrounding natural beauty are all part of a leisurely beach vacation.

Zadar gives nature enthusiasts the opportunity to experience the majestic magnificence of its national parks. A short boat ride will take you to the 89 desolate islands and islets of the Kornati National Park. Its rugged cliffs, clean waters, and plenty of marine life make it a paradise for sailors, divers, and outdoor enthusiasts. A well-liked destination for rock climbers and hikers, the area's Paklenica National Park also provides spectacular landscape, including karst formations, harrowing gorges, and deep woodlands.

Foodies enjoy Zadar's unique culinary scene. Many eateries in the city provide delicious food that is prepared using classic Mediterranean recipes and is renowned for its fresh seafood. Try regional delicacies like olives, cheeses, and wines while mixing with friendly locals at bustling local markets like the effervescent Zadar City Market.

Additionally, Zadar has a variety of cultural events all year long that celebrate its illustrious artistic and musical heritage. At St. Donat's Church, the Musical Evenings feature classical music in a beautiful setting, while the Zadar Summer Theatre Festival brings captivating plays to the city's historic locations.

In summary, Zadar stands out as a special location that masterfully combines its fascinating historical past with the wonders of nature and cutting-edge attractions. Every kind of traveler may find something to enjoy in the city, from its captivating old town to its exceptional architectural wonders, stunning coastline, and spectacular national parks. Thanks to its attractiveness, kindness, and vibrant cultural atmosphere, Zadar is a must-see destination that leaves an indelible imprint on the hearts of those who are fortunate enough to travel there.

ZAGREB

For travelers seeking the ultimate blend of endearing history, vibrant culture, and spectacular natural beauty, Zagreb, Croatia's capital and largest city, is a must-visit destination. Zagreb draws visitors from all over the world because to its intriguing history, stunning architecture, energetic atmosphere, and friendly locals.

One of the city's highlights is the Upper Town (Gornji Grad), Zagreb's historical center. The medieval section of this city is adorned with meandering cobblestone streets, quaint squares, and magnificent buildings. The beautiful Zagreb Cathedral and the famed St. Mark's Church, with its vibrantly tiled roof, both inspire amazement in visitors. While exploring the museums, art galleries, and charming shops in Upper Town, visitors may get a sense of the medieval atmosphere.

The Lower Town's (Donji Grad) beautiful 19th-century Austro-Hungarian architecture adds to the Upper Town's historical appeal. Ban Jelai Square, located in the heart of the city, is a popular meeting spot for both locals and tourists.

Indulge in some retail therapy in the lively Dolac Market, relax with a cup of coffee at one of the outdoor cafés, or just enjoy the area's wonderful architecture.

There are many different theaters, art galleries, and museums to explore in Zagreb, which has a vibrant and diverse cultural environment. By presenting personal stories and mementos from failed relationships, the unconventional attraction The Museum of Broken Relationships provides visitors an emotional and thought-provoking experience. High-caliber opera, ballet, and dramatic plays are presented by the Croatian National Theatre, while contemporary art by local and international artists is shown in the Museum of Contemporary Art.

Zagreb's parks and open spaces are a paradise for those who love the outdoors. There are peaceful walking trails, the Zagreb Zoo, and Maksimir Park, Southeast Europe's oldest public park. The exquisite Botanical Garden, a haven for plant enthusiasts, is near to the city center and includes a diversity of foreign flora. For panoramic city views, hiking trails, ski slopes in the winter, and the opportunity to explore the intriguing Medieval Fortress of Medvedgrad, visitors may climb Mount Medvednica.

It is well known that Zagreb has a strong cuisine culture. In the city, there are various eateries, coffee shops, and food carts selling anything from international cuisine to local Croatian cuisine. Visitors may experience local delicacies like kulen, a hot sausage, or trukli, a delicious pastry filled with cheese, as well as local wines like Graevina or Plavac Mali.

All throughout the year, Zagreb hosts a number of festivals and events that display its extensive cultural heritage. The Advent, a Christmas market that lasts a whole month, is highly well-liked in Zagreb. With brilliant lights, holiday decorations, and a variety of stalls offering crafts, food, and mulled wine, it transforms the city into a winter wonderland.

The INmusic Festival showcases performances by well-known international artists and attracts music lovers from all around the world.

Zagreb's convenient location in the middle of Europe makes it a fantastic starting place for exploring Croatia. From here, it's easy to go to the stunning Plitvice Lakes National Park, the Adriatic Sea islands, the coastal cities of Split and Dubrovnik, and other locations.

Visit the city of Zagreb, which offers a beautiful blend of history, culture, and natural beauty. No matter whether visitors choose to wander around the charming medieval alleys, immerse themselves in the vibrant cultural scene, or enjoy in the region's delectable cuisine, they will definitely be charmed by the seductive ambiance of this Croatian gem.

PULA

The Croatian city of Pula, which is located on the Istrian Peninsula, must be seen by visitors to this fascinating country. With its extensive history, stunning architecture, vibrant cultural scene, and exceptional natural beauty, Pula offers visitors from all over the world a unique experience.

One of Pula's main attractions is its Roman heritage. The Pula Arena is the most well-known monument in the city and is a well maintained Roman amphitheater. It was built in the first century AD and is one of the best-preserved amphitheaters in the world. It provides a glimpse into the majesty and spectacle of ancient Rome. Thanks to the many events it presently organizes, including concerts, film festivals, and reenactments of gladiator fights, the arena is a hive of activity.

In addition to the arena, Pula is the location of many more old Roman buildings. The Arch of the Sergii, the Temple of Augustus, and the Roman Forum are some of the city's finest examples of Roman architecture. Walking through Pula's streets is like going back in time as you find the remnants of this once powerful empire.

In addition to its Roman legacy, Pula offers a broad variety of cultural pursuits. The city is home to several museums, notably the Archaeological Museum of Istria, which has a large collection of local history artifacts. The Historical and Maritime Museum of Istria offers insight into Pula's maritime past, while the Museum of Contemporary Art features works of modern and contemporary art.

For lovers of theater and music, Pula hosts a variety of events throughout the year. The Pula Film Festival, one of Europe's oldest film festivals, attracts both international filmmakers and cinema fans. The Dimensions and Outlook music festivals are great places for aficionados of electronic music to join together for wonderful nights of dancing and delight. These events create a buzzing atmosphere that animates and motivates the city.

In and around Pula, there is a wealth of unspoiled natural beauty to be found. Along the city's coastline, there are a number of lovely beaches and secluded coves where you can relax and take in the warm Mediterranean sun. The Brijuni Islands, only a short boat ride from Pula, provide a tranquil sanctuary with stunning natural beauty and a wide variety of wildlife. Learn about the intriguing history and animals of these beautiful islands by exploring the national park, renting bicycles, or enrolling on a tour.

Another draw for travelers in Pula is the local cuisine. Istrian cuisine is known for its fresh ingredients and flavors from the Mediterranean. The city's restaurants provide a delectable range of seafood, truffles, olive oil, and regional wines. Traditional foods like Istrian prosciutto, fui pasta, and homemade Istrian pastries must be tried by food enthusiasts.

Pula offers a range of hotel options to suit the requirements of every guest. From basic guesthouses and private apartments to luxury hotels with stunning sea views, there is lodging to suit every taste and budget.

The strategic location of Pula also makes it an excellent starting point for exploring the rest of Istria. Rovinj and Pore, two gorgeous towns with their own special charms and attractions, are just a short drive away. You may also go farther into the Istrian countryside to appreciate the pastoral beauty of the region by visiting hilltop towns, vineyards, and olive groves.

In conclusion, Pula is a destination that travelers to Croatia must see. Because of its extensive Roman history, vibrant cultural scene, stunning natural settings, and mouthwatering cuisine, it is a wonderful place to visit. No matter whether you are into history, art, music, nature, or simply the laid-back Mediterranean lifestyle, Pula has something to offer everyone. Plan your trip to

Pula right now so that you may create lifetime memories.

ROVINJ

Tourists from all over the world now flock to the lovely hamlet of Rovinj, which is situated in Croatia along the stunning Adriatic coastline. Thanks to its quaint old town, magnificent natural beauty, and rich cultural heritage, Rovinj offers a truly unforgettable experience that captivates the senses and leaves a lasting impression.

The charming ancient town of Rovinj, which is situated on a small peninsula and surrounded by azure waters, is one of the city's most notable landmarks. The narrow, cobblestone alleyways wind through the maze of pastel-colored homes with flower-filled balconies and charming cafés. The centerpiece of the old town is the imposing Church of St. Euphemia, whose bell tower offers panoramic views of the city and the Adriatic Sea. While meandering through the narrow lanes, visitors may peruse boutique shops, art galleries, and traditional Istrian pubs where they can enjoy local delicacies and fine wines.

For those who like the great outdoors, Rovinj is a paradise. The terrain around the town is stunningly gorgeous, with clear streams, remote beaches, and heavily wooded regions. The nearby Golden Cape Forest Park, a haven for outdoor activity, has hiking and biking paths that weave through fragrant pine trees and lead to undiscovered coves and spotless beaches. The nearby islands of St. Andrew and Katarina are accessible by boat for adventure-seeking tourists, who may swim, snorkel, and sunbathe in secluded island paradises.

Rovinj is also known for its rich cultural heritage, which can be seen in its traditions, architecture, and cuisine. The town's long history, which stretches back to Roman times, is reflected in the variety of architectural styles, including Venetian Gothic, Renaissance, and Baroque. The town is home to a sizable number of museums and art galleries where visitors may find out about the local history and see works by local artists. Two well-known annual events in

Rovinj, the Rovinj Summer Music Festival and the Feast of St. Euphemia, allow visitors to completely immerse themselves in the vibrant local way of life.

Foodies will be drawn to Rovinj by its gastronomic delights. The community is widely renowned for its mouthwatering seafood, which is served in charming seaside restaurants and is daily harvested by local fishermen. Truffles, olive oil, and Istrian prosciutto are the major components of Istrian cuisine, which combines Central European and Mediterranean flavors. At modest taverns and elegant cafes that place an emphasis on seasonal, locally produced products and real flavors, visitors may go on a gastronomic journey while savoring regional delicacies and wines.

For each tourist, Rovinj offers a range of experiences and activities in addition to its natural and cultural attractions. Rovinj has activities to suit every taste and interest, whether it is sailing the Adriatic coast, diving and snorkeling to explore the underwater world, or just relaxing on one of the town's beautiful beaches.

In conclusion, Rovinj is a must-see destination for those seeking the perfect blend of unspoiled natural beauty, rich cultural heritage, and delectable cuisine. It is the ideal location for anyone looking for a real and unique experience because of its charming old town, magnificent natural surroundings, rich history, and kind hospitality. Everyone may find something to enjoy in Rovinj, whether they like the great outdoors, history, delectable food, or just want to relax. Prepare to be enchanted by the town's timeless beauty and enticing appeal when you plan your vacation to Rovinj.

SIBENIK

Every visitor should include sibenik, a quaint city on Croatia's breathtaking Adriatic coast, on their must-visit list. A unique experience that appeals to a range of interests is offered by Ibenik thanks to its rich history, magnificent architecture, breathtaking natural beauty, and hospitable Mediterranean atmosphere.

One of sibenik's top attractions, the St. James Cathedral, is recognized by UNESCO as a World Heritage Site. This architectural wonder, which was made entirely of stone, is a great example of human ingenuity and talent. A visit to the cathedral is essential for art and history enthusiasts because of its beautiful intricacy and superb sculptural decorations.

As you meander around the Old Town of Sibenik, you'll be entranced by its charming lanes as you take in the medieval atmosphere and immaculately kept buildings. The town's meandering cobblestone paths, ancient stairways, and hidden courtyards transport you back in time. Explore the city walls, stop at the ancient fortifications of St. Michael and St. Nicholas, then go to the peak for sweeping views of the Adriatic Sea.

Sibenik has a lot to offer outdoor enthusiasts. Just a short boat ride away lies the gorgeous Kornati National Park, an archipelago of 89 stunning islands. Due to its azure waters, soaring cliffs, and an abundance of marine life, the park is a snorkeler and diver's paradise. Visit the Krka National Park instead, which is well known for its gushing waterfalls and lush greenery. Swim in the clear waters or hike one of the park's numerous trails to truly experience nature's magnificence.

Sibenik also boasts a vibrant cultural scene. The International Children's Festival, which takes place every June, features the best performances of children's theater, music, and dance from across the world. The Sibenik Dance Festival and the Sibenik Street Music Festival are two other events that attract artists and performers from far and wide. Immerse yourself in the local arts and culture to get a deeper sense of the city.

Even the most sophisticated eaters will be pleased with Ibenik's gastronomic offerings. Take advantage of the area's fresh seafood offerings, which include grilled Adriatic fish, octopus salad, and black risotto with cuttlefish ink. If you drink a bottle of local Dalmatian wine with your dinner, you'll enjoy the real flavors of the Adriatic shore. Don't forget to try the legendary Sibenik liqueur, a city-produced herbal combination that has been produced for decades.

Sibenik has a certain appeal that comes from its kind and welcoming population. Their kindness and desire to share their traditions and experiences will make your stay even more unforgettable. You may have a better grasp of the city and its inhabitants via conversation and learning about their way of life.

Whether you like architecture, nature, culture, or cuisine, Ibenik offers a unique and diverse experience that appeals to everyone. Due to its historical landmarks, magnificent natural landscape, lively cultural scene, and warm hospitality, it is a must-visit spot for travellers seeking a true Croatian experience.

Chapter 2: Things to do

Swimming and sunbathing

With its lovely Adriatic Sea coastline, Croatia offers visitors a variety of activities. Among these, swimming and sunbathing are without a doubt two of the most popular, luring tourists from all over the world. Croatia provides the perfect setting for engaging in these enjoyable sports thanks to its clear waters, attractive beaches, and pleasant Mediterranean climate.

Swimming is fantastic in Croatia. The country is home to several beaches, each of which is exquisite in its own way. There are lively beach towns as well as tranquil coves to suit every taste. The tranquil, friendly waters of the Adriatic Sea are a dream for swimmers of all ability levels, whether you are a beginner or an experienced. Summertime swimming and leisurely dips are ideal when the water is at a pleasant temperature. The stunning blue color of the ocean enhances Croatia's appeal as a swimming destination.

One of Croatia's most well-known swimming spots is the Dalmatian coast. In cities like Split, Zadar, and Dubrovnik, there are many beautiful beaches where visitors can unwind and go swimming. Zlatni Rat (Golden Horn) and Dubovica Beach are two of the stunning beaches on the island of Hvar, which is well-known for its exciting nightlife and gorgeous surroundings. These beaches are fantastic for relaxing and swimming at. Further north, on the Istrian peninsula, there are stunning beaches like those in Rovinj and Pula where visitors may unwind in the sun and go swimming in the Adriatic.

Croatia is a total haven for sunbathers. The country provides sun worshipers with a broad selection of options thanks to its more than 1,000 islands. Depending on your desire, Croatia offers both sandy beaches and rocky shores. Long lengths of beaches with golden sand on the stunning Makarska Riviera, in the center of

Dalmatia, are very popular with tourists. The gorgeous beaches in Bol, Brela, and Omis are particularly beloved by sunbathers because they provide the perfect harmony of serenity and unspoiled beauty.

Along with the mainland, Croatia's islands provide unrivaled opportunities for sunbathing. The islands of Bra, Vis, and Korula have some of the most beautiful beaches in the Adriatic, where visitors may relax in the sun and take in the breathtaking scenery. The well-known Zlatni Rat Beach on the island of Bra is a must-visit spot for sunbathers due to its distinctive shape and crystal-clear waters. On the party-loving island of Pag, long stretches of sandy beaches let visitors relax and take in the warm Mediterranean sun.

To enhance the sunbathing experience, many Croatian beaches provide convenient amenities including beach chairs, umbrellas, and beachside cafés and restaurants. This makes it possible for visitors to thoroughly unwind and enjoy their time outdoors. Croatia's commitment to environmental preservation and cleanliness is shown by the country's immaculate beaches and clear waters, which contribute to the attractiveness of sunbathing there.

In conclusion, Croatia provides a distinctive swimming and sunbathing experience. Croatia's stunning coastline, clear waters, and lovely beaches make it the perfect site for participating in these activities. Whether you're searching for a tranquil swim or a sun-kissed tan, Croatia's various landscapes and alluring waters make it a great destination for beach lovers and water enthusiasts alike.

Hiking and Biking

Croatia offers a wealth of opportunities for outdoor enthusiasts to engage in activities like motorcycling and hiking thanks to its magnificent terrain and diverse natural attractions. Exploring Croatia's trails on foot or a bike promises to be an exciting and life-changing experience, regardless of whether you're a nature lover or an adventurer.

Hiking in Croatia will open up a wide range of breathtaking views, from wild seashore walks to jagged mountain summits. Trekkers may fully experience nature's splendor at a number of national parks around the country, including Plitvice Lakes National Park, Paklenica National Park, and Krka National Park.

Plitvice Lakes National Park, a UNESCO World Heritage site, is widely renowned for its network of connected lakes and cascading waterfalls. Hiking around the park's network of walkways allows visitors to see the vibrant colours and fascinating settings up close. The paths' varying degrees of difficulty cater to both casual walkers and intrepid explorers. As you wander through lovely trees and listen to the sound of running water, you may follow the wooden paths and bridges for an outstanding hiking experience.

Paklenica National Park in the Velebit mountain range is a haven for hikers seeking more challenging terrain. Several well marked paths will lead you through the park's steep slopes, lofty cliffs, and beautiful beech forests. For experienced hikers, the famed Premui track, a 50-kilometer track that offers breathtaking panoramic views of the surroundings, is a great choice.

Hikers who also wish to see the shoreline have a wonderful backdrop thanks to the Croatian islands. The island of Bra, for example, provides a superb hiking opportunity with Vidova Gora as its highest peak. Huge panoramas of the Adriatic

Sea and adjacent islands await hikers who reach the top.

Additionally, Croatia is a treat for bikers. The country's diverse landscape allows for a variety of bicycling experiences, from tranquil rides along the coast to exhilarating mountain biking trips.

The stunning roads and quaint settlements along the Croatian coast will appeal to cyclists greatly. On the northwest-facing Istrian Peninsula, a network of well-kept bike paths meanders past scenic villages, vineyards, and olive groves. You may experience delectable local cuisine and world-famous Istrian wines along the way, giving your bike adventure a gourmet touch.

The hinterland of Dalmatia may provide opportunities for mountain bikers. The tough terrain, which contains forested hills and winding roads, presents riders with a thrilling challenge. On trails that wind through the scenic Mosor and Biokovo mountain ranges, for example, cyclists may take in stunning views of the Adriatic shoreline in the vicinity of Split.

Croatia also hosts a lot of cycling races and events that attract athletes from all over the world. One notable event is the Istrian MTB race, which travels through the area's magnificent scenery and challenging terrain.

Whether you want to hike through Croatia's national parks, see its islands, or go horseback riding along the shoreline, this Mediterranean jewel provides a choice of scenic splendor and exhilarating activities. Croatia's diverse landscapes, agreeable climate, and rich cultural past entice outdoor enthusiasts looking to experience the wonders of hiking and riding.

Sailing and windsurfing

Sailing and windsurfing are two thrilling water activities that provide an incredible experience in the beautiful country of Croatia. Croatia has been a popular destination for sailors and windsurfers owing to its clear waters, stunning coastline, and favorable wind conditions. Whether you are an expert sailor or a beginner looking to try something new, Croatia offers a wide range of opportunities to participate in these exciting sports.

Croatian sailing provides the ideal setting for exploring the Adriatic Sea and all of its islands, coves, and hidden gems. Due to its more than a thousand islands, the Croatian coastline offers several chances for sailing trips. By hiring a sailboat or enrolling in a sailing expedition, you may discover secluded harbors, ancient coastal towns, and lively fishing villages. From the bustling ports of Split and Dubrovnik to the peaceful Kornati Islands, each location has its own unique appeal and beauty.

For its sailing routes, which provide the perfect blend of natural beauty and cultural heritage, the Dalmatian Coast is particularly well known. While floating down the coast, you could stop at famous places like Korula, which is said to be the birthplace of the famous explorer Marco Polo, or Hvar, which is famed for its vibrant nightlife and exquisite vineyards. Sailors are greeted by the calming tune of the Sea Organ as the charming city of Zadar and its neighboring islands provide a blend of historic structures and breathtaking scenery.

Anyone wishing for a riskier water sport in Croatia must learn how to windsurf. Windsurfing enthusiasts of all skill levels may take advantage of the nation's varied coastline and favorable wind patterns. In specialized windsurfing establishments, novice riders may get instruction from competent instructors while more experienced surfers can put their talents to the test with thrilling jumps and freestyle maneuvers.

Croatia's Istrian Peninsula is a well-liked windsurfing holiday destination because of its reliable winds and lovely beach communities. Locations like Rovinj and Pore are great for windsurfing since they have reliable winds and ample space to sail the waves. The consistent winds in Croatia's southern regions, such Bol and Viganj, draw windsurfers from all over the world.

One of the nicest things about sailing and windsurfing in Croatia is the accessibility of equipment and facilities. Along the coast, there are a lot of marinas and sailing schools that rent out boats, provide sailing lessons, and sell windsurfing equipment. Whether you like to rent a little dinghy or a luxurious yacht, there are options to fit every budget and taste.

Furthermore, Croatia's Mediterranean climate ensures optimal conditions for a variety of water activities with long, warm summers and mild winters. The best sailing and windsurfing conditions may be found from May to September, when pleasant temperatures and steady breezes provide for an enjoyable day on the water.

Croatia's coastline is home to breathtaking natural beauty and a rich cultural past in addition to the adrenaline of windsurfing and sailing. When you're not out on the water, you can explore ancient cities like Dubrovnik, Split, and Zadar, which include protected historical sites, bustling markets, and delectable local cuisine. Also accessible are the spectacular waterfalls and lush landscapes of the national parks Plitvice Lakes and Krka.

In conclusion, Croatia offers a wonderful opportunity for sailing and windsurfing enthusiasts to revel in the Adriatic Sea and its shoreline. Due to its many islands, strong winds, and lovely towns, Croatia is a refuge for both sailors and windsurfers. Whether you are an expert sailor or a beginner eager to learn, Croatia's alluring seas and magnificent scenery may help you create lifetime memories. Set sail on a thrilling tour across the breathtaking Croatian coastline by raising your sails, catching some wind, and doing so.

Visiting historical sites

Croatia is a country rich in history, with a plethora of intriguing historical landmarks luring travelers from all over the world. In addition to offering a view into Croatia's fascinating past, visiting these places is interesting and educational. Here are some amazing historical sites to see while in Croatia, ranging from well-preserved medieval towns to ancient remains.

One of Croatia's most important historical sites is the city of Dubrovnik. Dubrovnik, the "Pearl of the Adriatic," is well recognized for its remarkably well-preserved medieval walls. It is a UNESCO World Heritage Site. While wandering along these walls, you could be treated to breathtaking views of the city's red-roofed buildings and the shimmering Adriatic Sea. Within the city walls are several historic sites, including as the Rector's Palace, Sponza Palace, and the magnificent Gothic-Renaissance Dubrovnik Cathedral.

The beautiful Diocletian's Palace in Split is another intriguing historical site. This palace complex, which was built in the fourth century AD, is a functioning illustration of Roman architecture and engineering. While navigating its twisting passageways, you'll see antique columns, courtyards, and even an Egyptian sphinx. The Cathedral of St. Domnius in the palace is also a beautiful example of Romanesque and Gothic design.

Zagreb, the capital of Croatia, is located inland and has a considerable historical background as well. The Upper Town, also known as Gornji Grad, is where Zagreb's history is concentrated.

While meandering along cobblestone alleyways, seeing the iconic St. Mark's Church with its vibrantly tiled roof, and arriving there, you may tour the interesting Museum of Broken Relationships. The Lower Town, or Donji Grad, has a wide range of architectural designs, such as Art Nouveau and neoclassical structures like the Croatian National Theatre.

For everyone who is passionate in ancient history, a journey to Pula is a need. At Pula, a city on the Istrian Peninsula, you can view the Pula Arena, a beautifully preserved Roman amphitheater. This massive structure, which was previously used for gladiator fights, now accommodates concerts and other events. As you walk through, the enormous arches and stands let you to sense the weight of history.

As you go farther north, Zadar offers a distinctive combination of historic sites and beautiful scenery. A stunning example of Byzantine architecture can be seen in the medieval Church of St. Donatus, while Zadar's

Roman Forum showcases the remains of ancient temples and plazas. The Sea Organ and Sun Salutation, two modern pieces along the beach, provide a touch of contemporary art to the historic environment.

Last but not least, Trogir, a small Croatian town famous for its superb medieval architecture, is a UNESCO World Heritage Site. The historic core of Trogir is composed of a number of stunning stone buildings, including the ornate Romanesque and Gothic-styled Cathedral of St. Lawrence. The town is full with architectural marvels at every turn, creating the impression that you are going back in time.

Finally, seeing Croatia's historical sites offers a fascinating journey through time. The historical history of the country is fascinating and diverse, spanning from the Roman ruins in Pula to the medieval walls of Dubrovnik. By visiting these places, tourists may take in Croatia's rich history and discover more about its cultural significance. If you're interested in architecture, history, or simply want a different sort of holiday, Croatia's historical sites are sure to leave an impression.

Sampling the local cuisine

While the nation's breathtaking natural environment and historical attractions draw visitors from all over the world, one aspect that shouldn't be overlooked is its excellent cuisine scene. Trying Croatian cuisine is an essential since it will excite the palette and teach tourists more about the country's customs.

Croatian cuisine combines the delectable tastes of a number of its neighboring neighbors, including Italy, Austria, Hungary, and the Balkans. Since each region in Croatia has its own distinctive dishes and culinary specialties, it makes for a diverse and interesting holiday for food lovers. From hearty meat dishes to fresh seafood, Croatia's cuisine offers something for every palate.

One of the must-try delicacies to taste while traveling to a nation is the classic Croatian dish "peka," which is created by gently roasting meat, vegetables, and herbs underneath a bell-shaped top. During this prolonged cooking procedure, the ingredients are imbued with rich tastes, yielding meals that are creamy and delectable. Peka is a traditional Croatian meal that may be prepared with octopus, lamb, or veal. It is a memorable experience to eat it.

Seafood enthusiasts will find culinary heaven in Croatia. Due to its large coastline, the country has access to a plentiful supply of fresh seafood and shellfish. Seafood specialties that emphasize the abundance of the Adriatic Sea are available in the coastal towns and cities, such grilled sardines and octopus salad as well as black risotto made with cuttlefish ink. For a true taste of the Mediterranean, try "brudet," a flavorful fish stew made with tomatoes, onions, garlic, and white wine. Don't let it go by.

While traveling through the interior of Croatia, be sure to savor the hearty meat dishes that are a staple of the nation's cuisine. A popular kind of street food is the little grilled sausages known as "evapii," which are made from a blend of beef and pig. They are often served with "ajvar," a red pepper relish, and warm, freshly baked bread. Another well-liked treat is trukli, a traditional baked pastry filled with cottage cheese and often topped with sour cream. The combination of flavors and textures is incredible.

Take pleasure in some of Croatia's sweet treats to round off your culinary tour. "Kremnita," a vanilla and custard cream cake, is a popular treat in the majority of Croatian bakeries. The beach city of Dubrovnik is known for its "rozata," a creamy caramel custard with a hint of rose liqueur. These desserts, coupled with a variety of local pastries and fruit-based sweets, provide a delightful finish to any meal.

Croatian food is a fantastic opportunity to learn about the country's history, culture, and traditions while also indulging in some mouthwatering dishes. In numerous pubs and eateries around Croatia, visitors will discover a friendly atmosphere and kind locals willing to share their native food. Genuine hospitality, traditional music, and folk dances are often present throughout the dining experience, making it a really memorable one.

Additionally, visitors may learn more about the ingredients and preparation techniques that distinguish Croatian food by conversing with local farmers and producers at markets and culinary festivals. From the vibrant farmers' markets in Zagreb to the fish markets in Split, these places provide the opportunity to try the freshest regional products, including as olive oil, honey, cheeses, and wines.

In conclusion, everyone visiting Croatia should definitely sample the local cuisine. It is really delicious. From the interior to the beach towns, the variety and complexity of flavours will captivate your senses and leave a lasting impression.

Attending festivals and Events

Attending Festivals and Events to Learn About Croatia's Active Cultural Scene

In addition to having incredible natural beauty, Croatia also boasts a vibrant cultural scene that comes to life during its many festivals and events. It is a wonderful chance to completely experience Croatian culture and create lifetime memories by taking part in these thrilling events, which vary from historical recreations and traditional celebrations to music and film festivals. Let's look at the wide range of events and activities that make Croatia a must-visit destination for every serious traveler.

The majority of Croatia's events are undoubtedly music festivals. The country is well-known worldwide for holding captivating music events that entice tens of thousands of visitors each year. The renowned Ultra Europe event, which takes place in Split and draws followers of electronic music to watch performances by notable DJs, is one such occasion. A unique experience is created by the event's heart-pounding intensity and the gorgeous Adriatic Sea backdrop.

For lovers of classical music, the Dubrovnik Summer Festival offers a unique opportunity to attend outdoor performances among the city's landmarks. This well-known festival presents opera, theatre, and dance acts by combining local and international talents. The festival's spectacular finale is a breathtaking fireworks display that takes place above the ancient city walls, creating a romantic atmosphere.

Film fans can check out the Pula Film Festival, which is held in the city's ancient Roman amphitheatre. The chance to explore the world of film while luxuriating in the interesting locations is provided by this cinematic feast. It offers a wide range of international and Croatian movies. The event's open-air screenings under a starry sky seamlessly meld film and history.

Events abound to celebrate Croatia's lengthy historical history. The stunning horse show known as "The Battle of Sinj" is a recreation of a battle with the Ottoman Empire that took place in 1715. In a unique competition, knights compete while displaying their equestrian skill and remembering Croatia's glorious history. Viewers may go back in time and experience the excitement of the past thanks to this captivating event.

Traditional events may be used to display the folklore and customs of the country. The Rijeka Carnival, one of Europe's largest carnival festivities, lines the streets with colourful parades, costumed revellers, and cheerful music. This joyous celebration, which honours the spirit of fun and festivity, captivates both locals and tourists.

Additionally, Croatia's coastal regions have a number of marine-themed festivals to recognize the country's close links to the ocean. Both the

Komia Regatta on the island of Vis and the Brijuni Regatta in Pula are well-attended sailing events that attract competitors from all over the globe. These regattas provide opportunity to develop connections and pay respect to Croatia's marine tradition together with thrilling competition.

Croatia also holds a broad variety of regional festivals throughout the year in addition to these larger-scale celebrations and events. In Croatia's vibrant cultural milieu, there is always something happening, from traditional folk dances and religious processions to wine and gastronomic festivals that showcase the country's culinary specialties.

Festivals and events in Croatia provide visitors an opportunity to engage with locals, forge bonds that go beyond the typical tourist experience, and take in the rich cultural heritage of the nation. Whether it's via the pulsating rhythms of music festivals or the historical reenactments that transport you to bygone centuries, Croatia's festivals and events provide an unforgettable journey into the heart and soul of the country. Pack your bags and get ready to be enchanted by the rich tapestry of Croatian culture, one event at a time.

Chapter 3 : Where to stay

Hotels

Where to stay is one of the most important things to consider when making travel arrangements to Croatia. There are fortunately many of hotels to choose from, and each one has an own brand and charm. We'll examine some of Croatia's top hotels in this chapter, along with directions to get there.

Dubrovnik's Excelsior Hotel
The five-star Hotel Excelsior Dubrovnik is a lavish establishment with amazing views of the Adriatic Sea and a prominent position in the

heart of Dubrovnik. The hotel is at a great location for seeing the city since the old town is just a 15-minute walk away. To get to the hotel, take a taxi or shuttle from the airport in Dubrovnik.

Hotel Villa in Dubrovnik

Another prominent hotel in Dubrovnik is Villa Dubrovnik. This five-star hotel features beautiful sea views and is just a short walk from the city center. To get to the hotel, take a taxi or shuttle from the airport in Dubrovnik.

Hotel Lone

Five-star modern hotel Hotel Lone is located in the picturesque town of Rovinj and has opulent rooms with stunning views of the Adriatic Sea. You may fly into the airport in Pula and then take a taxi or shuttle to the hotel.

Hotel Bellevue in Dubrovnik

A five-star luxury hotel with breathtaking views of the Adriatic Sea, Hotel Bellevue Dubrovnik is positioned on a clifftop above the city. To get to the hotel, take a taxi or shuttle from the airport in Dubrovnik.

Cavtat Hotel in Croatia

Located in the charming hamlet of Cavtat and just a short drive from Dubrovnik, Hotel Croatia Cavtat is a five-star hotel with amazing views of the Adriatic Sea. To get to the hotel, take a taxi or shuttle from the airport in Dubrovnik.

Split Lav "Le Meridien"

"Le Meridien" A short distance from the city's heart, the five-star luxury hotel Lav Split in Split offers stunning views of the Adriatic Sea. To get to the hotel, take a taxi or bus from Split Airport.

Hotel Adriana in Hvar

The lovely five-star Hotel Adriana Hvar is located near to the main center on the island of Hvar and offers stunning sea views. From Split, you can take a ferry to Hvar, where you can then take a taxi or shuttle to get to the hotel.

Hotel Monte Mulini

A five-star luxury hotel with breathtaking seaviews, the Hotel Monte Mulini is located in Rovinj and is just a short walk from the town's core. You may fly into the airport in Pula and then take a taxi or shuttle to the hotel.

Hotel Amfora Grand Beach Resort

The five-star Hotel Amfora Grand Beach Resort on the island of Hvar is a stunning structure that offers amazing sea views and is near to the town center. From Split, you can take a ferry to Hvar, where you can then take a taxi or shuttle to get to the hotel.

Dubrovnik Palace Hotel

Just a short drive from the city center, the magnificent Hotel Dubrovnik Palace is a five-star hotel in Dubrovnik that is located on the Lapad Peninsula. It offers breath-taking sea vistas. To get to the hotel, take a taxi or shuttle from the airport in Dubrovnik.

Inn at Adriatic

The luxurious five-star Hotel Adriatic is located in the Peljeac Peninsula hamlet of Orebi. It is just a short stroll from the town center and offers stunning sea views. To get to the hotel, take a taxi or shuttle from the airport in Dubrovnik.

Park Hotel Split

Hotel Park Split, a five-star luxury hotel with amazing sea views, is situated in Split and only a short walk from the city center. To get to the hotel, take a taxi or bus from Split Airport.

Dubrovnik's Hotel Kompas
On the Lapad Peninsula in Dubrovnik, only a short drive from the city's center, sits the luxurious four-star Hotel Kompas Dubrovnik. It offers breath-taking sea vistas. To get to the hotel, take a taxi or shuttle from the airport in Dubrovnik.

Dubrovnik's Hotel Valamar Lacroma
A short distance from the city center, the sumptuous four-star Hotel Valamar Lacroma Dubrovnik is located on the Babin Kuk peninsula in Dubrovnik. It offers breath-taking sea vistas. To get to the hotel, take a taxi or shuttle from the airport in Dubrovnik.

Lone Hotel Rovinj

Located in the town of Rovinj and only a short walk from the city's center, Hotel Lone Rovinj is a five-star luxury hotel with breathtaking sea views. You may fly into the airport in Pula and then take a taxi or shuttle to the hotel.

Neptun Hotel Dubrovnik

The lavish four-star Hotel Neptun Dubrovnik offers beautiful views of the sea and is located on the Lapad Peninsula in Dubrovnik, only a short drive from the city center. To get to the hotel, take a taxi or shuttle from the airport in Dubrovnik.

Solin, hotel president

In the town of Solin, near to Split, the sumptuous four-star Hotel President Solin is located. It is just a short drive from the city center. It offers stunning coastal views. To get to the hotel, take a taxi or bus from Split Airport.

Apartments

While visiting Croatia, finding the appropriate apartment to stay in might really enhance your experience. Croatia is a lovely country known for its stunning coastline, historic cities, and rich cultural heritage. Whether you're visiting Dubrovnik, Split, Zagreb, or any other well-known location, your trip will be much more memorable if you choose the perfect apartment in the right location.

One of the first considerations while selecting an apartment in Croatia is the location. Croatia offers a variety of accommodations, including lovely seaside resorts and apartments in the heart of thriving towns. According to your preferences, you may choose an apartment that satisfies your needs and makes it easier for you to visit the neighboring attractions.

If you like seeing historical sites and beautiful medieval towns, renting an apartment in the

UNESCO-listed mediaeval Town of Dubrovnik can be a perfect choice. The narrow cobblestone streets, ancient city walls, and breathtaking views of the Adriatic Sea will take you back in time. The Dubrovnik Cathedral, the Rector's Palace, and the well-known Stradun promenade are all easily accessible from this advantageous location.

For travelers seeking a mix of history and nature, a Split apartment can be a fantastic option. The UNESCO-listed Diocletian's Palace stands out among Split's well-preserved Roman ruins as being the most remarkable and obvious. If you stay near to the palace, you may visit the Cathedral of St. Domnius, see its ancient halls, and enjoy the bustling atmosphere of the city's narrow streets.

If you desire a more urban setting, there are many different apartments to choose from in Zagreb, the city's capital. Zagreb has a bustling nightlife in addition to having a lot of museums and art galleries. You can reach Zagreb

Cathedral, Ban Jelai Square, and Upper Town's charming streets easily if you remain in the city center.

People seeking a relaxing beach holiday may choose from a large selection of apartments on the Dalmatian Islands, many of which have breath-taking sea views. The most well-known islands are Hvar, Brac, and Korcula, which are famous for their crystal-clear waters, secret coves, and charming towns. Choosing an apartment on one of these islands will allow you to relax in a peaceful environment while admiring the natural beauty of the Adriatic Sea.

No matter where you stay, Croatian apartments often provide a comfortable and enjoyable stay. Many apartments provide modern comforts including fully equipped kitchens, separate bathrooms, and comfortable bedrooms. They often provide complimentary Wi-Fi and air conditioning, making for a pleasant stay even during the stifling heat.

You have the opportunity to completely experience the local culture by renting an apartment. By renting an apartment in Croatia, a country known for its kind and welcoming people, you may get a taste of local life. You may interact with your neighbors, visit local markets, and even try your hand at preparing traditional Croatian dishes with seasonal ingredients.

Finally, finding the appropriate accommodation in Croatia might really enhance your experience. Croatia offers a range of options to suit different tastes, whether you choose for a tranquil coastal retreat or a central location in the heart of a historic city. By choosing an apartment in a fantastic location, you can easily discover the region's attractions, immerse yourself in the culture, and create lifetime memories of your holiday to this lovely Mediterranean country.

Hostels

Croatia is a well-known tourist destination for travelers from all over the world because of its stunning beaches, vibrant cities, and rich cultural heritage. One of the best ways to see the country's splendor without going over budget is to stay in hostels. Croatia boasts a wide range of hostels, from budget-friendly places to stylish boutique places, allowing visitors to take in the breathtaking surroundings while benefiting from easy and affordable accomodation. This book highlights the best hostels in Croatia's popular tourist destinations, ensuring that every guest has a good stay.

Dubrovnik, known as the "Pearl of the Adriatic," is renowned for its lovely old town and intact medieval defenses. Hostel Angelina Old Town is a popular choice among backpackers due to its ideal location inside the historic walls, lovely dorm rooms, and inviting common areas. The experience is more upscale with Fresh* Sheets. Elegant private rooms and a terrace with views of the ancient town are also features of the Kathedral Dubrovnik.

Split
Split is a flourishing beach city with Roman-era buildings and a lively vibe. The beautiful Tchaikovsky Hostel provides a warm atmosphere, spacious accommodations, and a prominent location near to the Diocletian's Palace in the heart of Split. Another excellent option is the Golly & Bossy Design Hostel, known for its chic interior design and visitor-friendly social events.

Croatia's Zadar, on the Dalmatian coast, is well known for its breathtaking sunsets and Roman ruins. The Boutique Hostel Forum stands out as a great choice since it is adjacent to the famous Sea Organ and offers well furnished rooms. An option is The Lazy Monkey Hostel, which provides a relaxed atmosphere with a large garden and a cozy common space.

Natural beauty Plitvice Lakes National Park has blue lakes and cascading waterfalls. It is a place that is recognized by UNESCO. Backpackers passing through the area will find shelter at the Falling Lakes Hostel, which has a cozy atmosphere made of wood, a friendly staff, and quick access to hiking routes. The guesthouse-style Villa Mukinja, which boasts pleasant rooms and a tranquil garden, is a fantastic option.

Croatia's vibrant city, Zagreb, offers a unique fusion of historic landmarks and contemporary art. With its modern decor, lively bar, and variety of rooms, The Swanky Mint Hostel stands out as a true hostel experience. The Funk Lounge Hostel, which is in the heart of the city, impresses visitors with its unique style and lively social scene.

Hvar: The picturesque Adriatic Sea island of Hvar attracts visitors in search of stunning beaches and a buzzing nightlife. A short walk from Hvar's main square, Hostel Marinero offers comfortable dormitories and helpful staff. The White Rabbit Hostel is another popular choice; it features a laid-back atmosphere, spacious common areas, and a sunny terrace.

Because of its magnificent natural beauty and intriguing cities, Croatia is a must-visit destination, and staying in hostels ensures affordable and enjoyable accommodation. Whether you want to experience the waterfalls at the Plitvice Lakes, unwind on the beaches of Hvar, or explore the ancient city of Dubrovnik, there is a hostel to suit your needs. By selecting from the many hostels available around Croatia, you may have an authentic experience, meet new people, and create budget-friendly memories.

Camping

For those who like being in nature, camping in Croatia offers a very unique experience. Croatia provides a range of diverse settings, from stunning national parks to wonderful shoreline locations, making it the ideal location for an outstanding camping experience. This article will look at some of Croatia's best camping spots, highlighting their unique features and allurements that make them must-see destinations for every enthusiastic traveler.

National Park of the Lakes in Plitvice

A UNESCO World Heritage Site, the Plitvice Lakes National Park is known for its stunning rushing waterfalls and emerald-colored lakes. It is located in central Croatia. Camping within the park's boundaries allows visitors to awaken to the peaceful sounds of nature while being surrounded by lovely trees and a wide variety of wildlife. Given that it features tidy campsites and limited amenities, the park is an excellent destination for those who appreciate the outdoors. A boat ride over the park's lakes or a leisurely walk along its network of trails both provide close-up views of its otherworldly splendor.

National Park of Paklenica

At the southernmost tip of the Velebit Mountain Range, Paklenica National Park enchants campers with its stunning canyons and dramatic karst landscapes. There are designated camping areas in the park that may meet a range of requirements, from basic tent sites to facilities for campers and caravans. Because of its challenging rock climbing routes, attractive hiking trails, and opportunity to explore rare flora and fauna, Paklenica is a well-liked vacation spot for thrill seekers. Due to the park's proximity to the sea, campers may combine mountain activities with a refreshing dip in the Adriatic Sea.

Krka National Park

Southern Krka National Park in Croatia enchants visitors with its stunning waterfalls and lush surroundings. Camping adjacent to the park offers a great opportunity to experience the tranquility of the natural world. Modern conveniences are offered at the campgrounds, and visitors are free to explore the park's numerous routes that lead to breathtaking landscapes and gushing waterfalls. Swimming in the emerald-colored pools under the renowned Skradinski Buk waterfall is a favorite activity for many campers. Additionally, the park offers boat cruises that take visitors to Visovac, a lovely island that is adorned with a centuries-old Franciscan monastery.

National Park Kornati
Kornati National Park provides a pristine haven for anybody searching for an off-the-grid camping experience with its abundance of isolated islands, islets, and reefs. Campers and boaters will find this islands, which can only be accessible by boat, to be a delight. By camping in designated areas like Levrnaka or Vrulje,

spending peaceful nights under the stars, and exploring secluded coves and stunning beaches during the day, visitors can fully appreciate the park's untainted beauty. Naturalists will love Kornati because snorkeling and scuba diving there reveal a vibrant underwater environment teeming with marine life.

Croatia's camping areas provide a broad range of landscapes and experiences for travelers wishing to reestablish a connection with nature and embark on unforgettable expeditions. Whether it's the captivating waterfalls of Plitvice Lakes National Park, the spectacular canyons of Paklenica National Park, the serene serenity of Krka National Park, or the remote islands of Kornati National Park, each location provides a unique and immersive camping experience. Along with hiking,mountain climbing and swimming.

Chapter 4: Where to eat

Restaurant

Croatia is not just a paradise for history and sun lovers, but it is also a gourmet delight with its stunning Adriatic Sea beachfront and rich cultural heritage. A peculiar combination of influences from the Mediterranean, Central Europe, and the Balkans can be found in the nation's food, creating a diverse gourmet environment. Croatia offers a wide range of flavors to tantalize your palate, from traditional fish dishes to hearty meat specialties and decadent desserts. Here is a list of some of Croatia's top restaurants that travelers looking for the best dining experiences may want to consider checking out.

360° - Dubrovnik: Located within the Old Town's ancient walls, this restaurant offers breathtaking views of the Adriatic Sea and the city's crimson roofs. There are undoubtedly highlights on the menu at this Michelin-starred restaurant, with dishes like octopus carpaccio and black risotto.

The charming seaside resort of Rovinj is home to Monte, another Michelin-starred gem. The restaurant serves modern Croatian cuisine with a focus on seasonal, fresh ingredients and inventive cooking techniques. Monte offers delicious culinary delights like sea bass with squid ink gnocchi and pastries flavoured with lavender.

Pelegrini in the historic city of Sibenik offers a first-rate dining experience and is housed in a palace from the 15th century. The restaurant delivers traditional Dalmatian flavours with a modern twist, such as Adriatic fish with wild asparagus and pasta with truffle infusions. The wine selection is similarly outstanding and features the best Croatian wines.

Bokeria Kitchen & Wine Bar in Split is a trendy eatery that is located in the city's heart. The restaurant's menu include dishes like grilled octopus, delicious pasta, and delectable steaks that mix international and Mediterranean flavours. The stylish furnishings and lively atmosphere improve the whole experience.

Nav in Dubrovnik has spectacular views of the city's ancient harbour and is tucked away in the charming neighbourhood of Pole. Fish carpaccio, lobster, and oysters are just a few of the meals that use fresh seafood prominently on the menu. The terrace seating area allows guests to enjoy the stunning surroundings.

Zagreb's Zinfandel's is a fine-dining establishment famous for its appealing ambiance and excellent cuisine. It is located within the well-known Esplanade Hotel in Zagreb. The emphasis of the cuisine is on seasonal ingredients and modern interpretations of classic Croatian meals. A large selection of domestic and foreign brands are available in the wine cellar.

Concealed within Split's renowned Diocletian's Palace, Konoba Stari Grad offers a cozy setting and typical Dalmatian cuisine. Traditional dishes on the menu include grilled sardines, homemade pastas, and peka (slow-cooked meat and vegetables). The welcoming courtyard is a great place to dine outside.

The opulent Nautika restaurant in Dubrovnik is housed in a 19th-century stone castle and is conveniently situated near the Pile Gate. Meals like scallops with truffle foam and Adriatic lobster, which combine fresh seafood with avant-garde flavours, are on the menu. The balcony offers views of the sea and Dubrovnik's famed old walls.

In the centre of the city lies the renowned restaurant Vinodol, which serves both Croatian and international cuisine. Along with seafood and meat dishes, the menu offers a variety of alternatives, such as gluten-free and vegetarian selections, the friendly atmosphere and timely service.

Taverns

Taverns, or "konobas" in Croatian, are traditional eateries where guests may try local cuisine and immerse themselves in the vibrant local culinary scene. The following list includes some of Croatia's top eateries where you may have a wonderful meal:

. Konoba Menego (Dubrovnik): This charming eatery is located in the heart of the Old Town and is renowned for its fresh seafood and traditional Dalmatian dishes. Try the grilled fish dishes or the restaurant's renowned black risotto.

Konoba Stari Grad (Split) offers a cozy setting and a menu filled with Mediterranean dishes within the historic Diocletian's Palace. Don't miss out on their slow-cooked lamb peka, which is served with a bell-shaped top.

The family-run restaurant Konoba Fetivi in Rovinj serves traditional Istrian cuisine with a modern twist. Enjoy their homemade pasta, local wines, and dishes flavored with truffles.

Konoba Mate offers a warm atmosphere and wide-ranging views of the Adriatic Sea on the island of Korula. Try their freshly caught seafood, octopus salad, and traditional peka dishes.

Inconspicuous Konoba Nikola is a restaurant in Zagreb's Upper Town that provides authentic Croatian cuisine. For dessert, try their homemade strudel, roast pig's knuckles, and hearty goulash.

Because of its kind, welcoming staff and comforting fare, Ibenik's Konoba Vinko is a must-visit pub. Profit from their grilled meats, local cheeses, and real Ibenik rafioli for a sweet pleasure.

The beach town of Pula is home to Konoba Batelina, a sanctuary for seafood lovers. The menu features a range of dishes made with freshly caught fish and shellfish that have an emphasis on both quality and simplicity.

The Konoba Morgan restaurant on the island of Hvar offers a relaxed atmosphere and delectable regional food. Use their seafood platters, seasoned anchovies, and famous Hvar wines to your advantage.

Located in the historic city of Zadar, Konoba Bako enchants visitors with genuine Dalmatian food and kind service. It's worth sampling the grilled meats, silky seafood risotto, and excellent bread.

The ancient tavern Konoba Dida in Dubrovnik is well known for its hearty fare and stunning views. It is situated nearby Dubrovnik in the quaint village of Bosanka. Don't pass up the lamb that was roasted inside an iron bell.

On the island of Bra, Konoba Nono offers a homey atmosphere and food that emphasizes regional specialties. Try their grilled lamb, fresh octopus, and renowned Bra cheese.

Konoba Mondo (Pore): This eatery combines conventional cooking techniques with regional Istrian food. It is situated in the port city of Pore. Take advantage of their grilled meats, truffle-flavored pasta, and local wines.

Konoba Feral is situated in the newly renovated 14th-century building in Korula town.

Pizzerias

Pizza lovers will discover several traditional Croatian recipes, which also include international flavors. Many pizzerias can be found in Croatia, which will appeal to those seeking an Italian flavor. To ensure that a wonderful slice of pizza completes your culinary experience, this guide will examine some of Croatia's top pizzerias and their locations.

Our pizza adventure begins in Zagreb, the vibrant city of Croatia. There are several excellent pizzerias in Zagreb, which is renowned for its beautiful architecture and energetic atmosphere. Pizzeria O'Hara, located in the heart of the city, offers a wide variety of delicious pizzas with both traditional and modern toppings. If you like a welcoming, family-run establishment, Pizzeria Karijola, known for its authentic Neapolitan-style pizzas, is a must-visit.

Coastal Snacks

As we go down the beautiful Croatian coastline, there are several pizzerias that provide fantastic sea views in addition to delicious pizza. In Zadar's historic center, Pizzeria Gusti serves delectable wood-fired pizzas that you won't soon forget. While Pizzeria Galija offers a friendly atmosphere and a wide assortment of pies, Pizzeria Bokamorra stands out for its creative and sophisticated pizza offerings in Split.

As our journey continues, we reach Dubrovnik, a charming city known for its ancient fortifications and breathtaking surroundings. Pizzeria Mirakul brings a bit of paradise here with their thin-crust pizzas made with organic ingredients and stunning views of the Adriatic Sea. Pizzeria Tabasco offers a superb selection of pizzas and a warm environment for a lovely and intimate experience. It is hidden away in the Old Town's twisting passageways.

The Untravelled Route

Pizza fans shouldn't miss Croatia's undiscovered gems, which are found away from the popular tourist destinations. Visitors are won over by the original wood-fired pizzas created with affection and served in a welcoming setting at Pizzeria Da Sergio in the charming hamlet of Rovinj. Pizzeria Nono, located in the northern region of Istria, serves a broad variety of creative pizzas that often use regional truffles, a delicacy of the region.

island vacations

For pizza with a view, Croatia's gorgeous islands are the ideal setting. On the island of Hvar, the Pizzeria Jurin offers a selection of wood-fired pizzas together with breathtaking Adriatic views. On Vis Island, which is well-known for its natural beauty and where Pizzeria Dionis is situated, you may have freshly made pizzas while soaking in the tranquility of the location.

Thanks to its unique culinary environment, Croatia welcomes guests with open arms and offers a vast range of pizzerias to explore. Every pizzeria offers a unique experience and the chance to savour delectable pizzas, whether it is in the bustling streets of Zagreb or the quaint coastal towns and peaceful island retreats. Whether you like a classic Margherita or a refined variant, the pizzerias in Croatia are ready to satisfy your cravings. So, while planning your trip to Croatia, be sure to include a visit at one of these pizzerias and let the Italian flavours mingle with the scenery.

Bars

For travelers seeking a vibrant nightlife where they may delight in a pleasant atmosphere, exquisite drinks, and lifelong friendships, there are numerous bars all around the country. From well-known coastal towns to hidden gems tucked away in charming villages, Croatia offers a broad selection of pubs to satisfy every taste. Here are some of the top locations and their operating hours to assist you on your Croatian bar-hopping tour.

1. Dubrovnik: A UNESCO World Heritage Site, Dubrovnik is renowned for its stunning Old Town and historic defences. When it comes to bars, there are many charming taverns, stylish cocktail clubs, and busy pubs to pick from. The well-known Buza Bar, which is elevated on cliffs outside the city walls and offers

breathtaking views of the Adriatic Sea, is a must-visit. Numerous pubs in Dubrovnik stay open late because of the city's vibrant nightlife.

2. Split: Split, Croatia's second-largest city, is renowned for its bustling seafront promenade and ancient Roman ruins. Along the Riva, there are several taverns and cafés that provide delicious regional food and enjoyable drinks. The Hemingway Bar, which offers a wide variety of drinks and a sophisticated ambience, is a well-liked alternative. Most bars in Split remain open until quite early in the morning, allowing for a lively and unforgettable experience.

3. Hvar: Hvar Island is a favourite pick for tourists looking for both breathtaking natural landscape and a vibrant nightlife. Numerous trendy bars and clubs can be found in the town of Hvar, which attracts a wide range of patrons. Carpe Diem is well-known for its beachfront setting and exciting activities that go far into the night on a lonely island off the coast of Hvar.

4. Zadar: Zadar is a historical city with a nice promenade along the coastline and a great old town. There are several bars in the city that may satisfy every taste. The Garden Lounge Bar is a well-liked hangout because of its relaxed atmosphere, live music, and invigorating cocktails. Most bars in Zadar open early in the evening and close around midnight, making for the perfect balance of a wild night out and a relaxing night in.

5. Rovinj: Rovinj is a quaint coastal town with colourful houses and cobblestone streets. The bars and cafés in the town, which provide a lovely blend of historical charm and contemporary design, are infused with the vibrant energy of the community. With stunning views of the sun setting and an extensive drink menu, The Valentino drink & Champagne Bar stands out. The majority of Rovinj's pubs close around midnight or later during the peak tourism period.

6. Zagreb: The capital city of Croatia, Zagreb, boasts a thriving and varied bar scene. The city's Lower Town is a hub of activity, with a number of eateries and bars offering a range of drinks and entertainment options. Hemingway Bar, the most well-liked bar in the area, is renowned for its classy ambiance and top-notch beverages. Many Zagreb pubs open in the early evening and stay open until the early hours of the morning, especially on the weekends.

7. Pula: Situated on the Istrian Peninsula, Pula is well-known for its gorgeous beaches and its surviving Roman amphitheatre. You may unwind at one of the numerous bars or pubs in the city after a long day of exploring. The Uljanik Bar, housed in a former shipyard, is a popular choice since it offers a unique industrial ambiance and a wide selection of beverages. Bars in Pula often stay open late, especially during the summer.

It's important to keep in mind that opening hours may vary depending on the season and the specific company. The majority of pubs in Croatia open in the early evening and remain open until late at night, however some may have different hours.

Chapter 5: Budgeting

Transportation

Numerous factors, including transportation, must be considered while planning a trip to Croatia. Whether you're visiting historic cities, lazing in the sun on the Adriatic coast, or seeing the scenic countryside, planning your transportation budget is essential. This comprehensive guide aims to provide you sound guidance on how to use Croatia's transportation system while minimizing your expenses.

1. Research Croatia's transportation options before your trip to be prepared. Find out about the various modes of transportation, such as taxis, ferries, buses, and trains. Investigate the routes, times, and prices to make informed decisions. A wonderful source to get up-to-date information is online websites and travel message boards.

2. Consider Regional Variations: Croatia is divided into numerous regions, each of which has different transportation requirements. In large cities like Split, Dubrovnik, and Zagreb, there are well-developed transportation networks that include buses, trams, and local trains. Since there may not be many public transit options in smaller towns and rural areas, other arrangements would be needed.

3. Using public transportation is a sensible and cost-effective method to go across cities and between large towns. Buses connect different parts of the country and are the most often used kind of public transportation. Longer trips cost more, although rates are often reasonable. Buy tickets at designated kiosks, ticket machines, or other sites, or from the driver.

4. Croatian Railways: The Republic of Croatia's railway network connects the major cities and offers a stunning form of transportation. Despite moving more slowly than buses, trains nonetheless provide a comfortable and scenic

experience. Check the train schedules in advance, especially for long-distance routes, and consider purchasing tickets online to receive the best deals.

5. Island Hopping and Ferries: Croatia's coastline is dotted with beautiful islands, making them a must-see destination. Ferries and catamarans that transport passengers to other islands provide regular services. Budget-conscious travelers should account for the possibility that island hopping may be more expensive at the height of the summer.

6. Renting a vehicle in Croatia allows you flexibility and convenience, particularly if you wish to deviate from the beaten path or visit remote areas. Compare prices from several rental providers to get the best deals, and book in advance. Be aware of additional costs like parking, tolls, and insurance. It's important to keep in mind that driving in cities may be challenging due to traffic and a shortage of parking.

7. Ridesharing and Taxis: In Croatia's main cities, ridesharing services like Uber and Bolt have taken the role of conventional taxis. They may be more affordable and provide upfront pricing for shorter journeys or larger groups. Taxis may be more expensive, even though they are often available, especially in tourist regions. Before entering, always make sure the metre is on or that a fee has been set.

Walking and cycling are enjoyable and inexpensive hobbies in Croatia because of the country's small-town feel and lovely landscapes. Numerous towns have bike-sharing programs, and renting bicycles is a typical method to explore islands and coastal areas. Use pedestrian-friendly areas and promenades, especially in historic cities, to get a sense of the local feel.

9. Budgeting Tips:
a. Make a well-considered strategy to save unnecessary transportation costs.

b. Consider purchasing discounted multi-day or local transit passes.

c. Travel during the off-peak seasons (spring or autumn) to avoid paying inflated prices.

d. Be flexible with your travel dates to take advantage of cheaper airfare.

e. Select regional, family-run hotels near to transit hubs to save down on travel expenses.

Accommodation

It's important to carefully consider your housing options and create a budget that works for you. This information aims to provide you enlightening details and practical guidance on how to effectively arrange your housing budget in Croatia.

1. Set a budget: Before embarking on any holiday, it's crucial to establish a manageable spending limit. Consider the length of your stay, your intended destinations, and the kind of lodgings you want. Prior to flying to Croatia,

decide how much you are willing to spend every night since there are various lodging options, from luxurious resorts to affordable hostels.

2. Research and comparison: Use online tools and travel websites to compare different hotel possibilities in Croatia. Review items, evaluate costs, and look for offers or reductions. This will provide you more information about average costs and assist you to make an informed decision.

3. Consider traveling in the shoulder season: The summer is Croatia's busiest vacation season, particularly in well-known cities like Dubrovnik and Split. Consider going in the shoulder seasons (spring and autumn) to enjoy lower hotel expenses. Not only will you save money, but you'll also get to enjoy nicer weather and less crowds.

4. Opt for self-catering lodging: If you want to reduce your food expenses, consider renting a self-contained apartment or holiday home. In

these options, which often feature a kitchenette or a full kitchen, you may prepare your own meals, saving you money on expensive restaurant bills.

5. Look into other locations: Croatia offers a number of wonderful coastal towns and islands, and although well-known destinations like Dubrovnik and Hvar may be pricey, there are numerous untapped gems that provide less priced options. Think about visiting places like Zadar, Rovinj, or the islands of Cres and Vis that offer more affordable accomodation.

6. Adopt the hostel lifestyle. Hostels are a terrific choice for budget-conscious tourists, particularly those who are alone travelers or who wish to connect with other adventurers. Many Croatian hostels provide clean, comfortable housing at a fraction of the cost of hotels. Look for hostels with excellent reviews and in convenient places.

7. Consider private rooms or guesthouses, which are a popular alternative to hotels in Croatia and are frequently referred to as "sobe" (guesthouses). They provide a more intimate and real experience, and many are more reasonably priced than traditional hotels. In general, these hotel alternatives are available, especially in more charming cities and villages.

8. Keep an eye out for any last-minute deals, promotions, or special offers that hotels, hostels, or other accommodations could be running. There are various locations that offer reduced rates for longer stays or for certain times of the year. By joining social media groups, following travel discussion forums, and subscribing to newsletters, you can stay up to date on these offers.

9. Consider camping: If you like outdoor activities, camping in Croatia may be a fantastic, cost-effective option. The country offers a broad variety of campsites in beautiful locations along the coast and in national parks. Being closer to

nature is an added benefit, and camping is sometimes far less expensive than traditional accommodation.

10. Retain your flexibility: Being flexible with your travel dates might sometimes result in significant savings. Consider altering your itinerary to take advantage of less expensive hotels or visit less busy locations. By reacting to the available options, flexibility helps you to get the most out of your money.

Making a Croatia vacation budget requires careful planning and research, to sum up. By establishing a prudent spending strategy.

Food

Croatia is a fascinating travel destination with beautiful landscape, an intriguing history, and delectable cuisine. Travelers need to budget their money wisely, especially for meals. You may indulge in Croatia's food without going overboard if you manage your money wisely. In this book, we'll look at a variety of tips and tricks that might help you make the most out of your food budget while seeing this beautiful country.

1. Become familiar with the local cuisine before beginning your journey. Try regional specialties like cevapi (grilled sausages), peka (a meal of slow-cooked pork and vegetables), and fresh seafood along the Adriatic coast. Knowing the traditional meals can help you locate affordable substitutes and make sensible judgments.

2. Make a meal plan. By organizing your meals in advance, you may save time and money. To prepare yourself for the day, think about eating a full breakfast and a light lunch. Due to their affordable daily menus or lunch specials, several eateries provide fantastic lunch options. Dinner alternatives include sitting down to a meal at a restaurant or shopping for fresh goods at neighboring markets.

3. Due to its breathtaking surroundings, Croatia is a picnicker's heaven. Visit your area to purchase groceries, fresh produce, local cheeses, cured meats, and bread. By bringing a picnic basket, you may save money while taking in the gorgeous environment while eating outdoors.

4. Street Food Gems: Croatian food is amazing and affordably priced. Find local food stalls or kiosks that serve classic goodies like burek (a savory pastry stuffed with cheese, meat, or vegetables), fritule (little doughnut-like pastries), and langos (fried bread with various toppings). These delicious snacks provide a quick and affordable option to eat to keep energized while traveling.

5. Discover Local Markets: You must visit local markets when visiting Croatia. Fresh fruits, vegetables, cheeses, olives, and other local specialties are all readily accessible. Interacting with local vendors may also provide insights into Croatian culture and food. Don't be afraid to

negotiate for a fair price since this is a part of markets occasionally.

6. Dine Like a Local: To reduce food prices, eat where the locals do. Step beyond the tourist areas to find affordable, family-run restaurants serving authentic Croatian cuisine. Along with saving money, you'll get a real experience and maybe even meet some new individuals.

7. Adopt the Konoba Culture: Konobas, the traditional Croatian taverns, provide hearty, home-cooked meals. These eateries are well known for offering a lot of food at reasonable prices. The environment is often welcoming and cozy, providing a fantastic opportunity to try local food without breaking the wallet.

8. Make Wise Beverage Choices: While exploring Croatia, remember to stay hydrated and make wise beverage decisions. Since tap water is often safe to drink, choose that over bottled water. Instead of buying bottled water, carry a reusable bottle with you and fill it up as

needed during the day. Additionally, while dining out, local wines should be considered since they are often affordable and of excellent quality.

9. Avoid Tourist Traps: Popular tourist destinations and attractions can have higher prices than neighborhood shops. Even while it is great to visit these places, consider venturing outside of the well-known tourist spots to find more affordable dining options. By visiting less well-known areas, you could come across unknown culinary pleasures.

10. Kitchen Facilities: If your accommodations include a kitchen, utilize it. The money you will spend dining out will be less if you buy groceries.

Activities

Having a well-thought-out budget is crucial to making the most of your trip, whether you're planning a relaxing beach getaway or an active exploration of its natural wonders. In this guide, we'll offer you some wise counsel and practical suggestions to assist you in setting a budget for your visit to Croatia's tourist sites.

1. Free and Low-Cost Activities: Croatia offers a variety of free and low-cost activities that allow you to fully appreciate the culture and natural beauty of the nation. Visit public parks, beaches, and historical sites that are free to access. Look into your neighbourhood markets, where you may benefit from the vibrant atmosphere and affordable local cuisine. Some popular low-cost pastimes include cycling, swimming, and hiking.

2. A lot of the stunning national parks and wildlife reserves in Croatia have an entrance fee. Make sure to do some research on the parks you want to visit and budget for entry fees, tour guides, and transportation between sites. Three well-known parks are Paklenica, Krka, and Plitvice Lakes. Consider visiting at a slower time of day when admission may be less expensive.

3. Cultural and Historical Attractions: Croatia is home to a wealth of historical and cultural landmarks. While some attractions require a fee, many provide discounted tickets for students, the elderly, or families. Make sure to plan your trips properly to take advantage of these discounts. You could get a deeper understanding of Croatia's history by visiting historical sites, museums, and art galleries.

4. Water activities: Kayaking, snorkelling, and diving are just a few of the water activities that are perfect for Croatia's stunning coastline and crystal-clear waters. Find out how much it will cost to take a guided tour or to rent some gear. Consider making bookings for your activities in advance for better price and availability. If money is tight, choose a few water activities that you really must undertake and give them high priority.

5. Festivals and Events: To emphasise its rich cultural history, Croatia hosts a multitude of

festivals and events all year round. While some events may not need tickets, others could. After doing some research on the festivals happening when you are there, create a budget for the ones you want to go to. It may be a wonderful experience and help you better understand the local culture to attend cultural events.

6. Souvenirs and Shopping: Purchasing trinkets and shopping while travelling may be enjoyable, but it's important to adhere to your spending plan to avoid overspending. Instead of buying souvenirs at well-known sites, look into small markets and shops where you could find unique and affordable goods. In Croatia, negotiating prices is customary, therefore don't be averse to doing so. Consider the weight and size of your items if you wish to travel light or have limited luggage space.

7. Guided Tours: If you're interested in taking a guided tour to see a certain location or collection of landmarks, research different tour providers and compare costs. It could be less expensive to

take a vacation with a group than a single one. However, to ensure a high-quality experience, read reviews and choose reputable operators.

8. Currency Exchange and Payment Options: Before your trip, familiarize yourself with the Croatian Kuna (HRK) and exchange some money. Although credit cards are often accepted, especially in tourist areas, it is always a good idea to have extra cash on hand for smaller establishments and local markets that may not accept cards. Beware of overseas transaction costs, and consider alerting your bank about your travel plans to avoid any card issues.

9. Travel Insurance: Having travel insurance that covers lost baggage, trip cancellations, and medical emergencies is essential. Even though it may seem like an unnecessary expenditure, it might save you from having to pay a lot of money in the case of unplanned events. Compare several insurance providers to get an insurance plan that fits your needs and price range.

10. Seasonal Factors: There are numerous tourist seasons in Croatia, with the summer months being the busiest and when prices are often higher. If you're looking to save money, think about going in the shoulder seasons (spring or autumn), when prices are often lower and crowds at popular attractions are reduced. Consider your options carefully since certain amenities or attractions could only be accessible during off-peak hours.

11. Prioritization and Flexibility: It's crucial to give priority to the occasions and pursuits that are most important to you, and to be adaptable with your financial situation. Budget your money wisely, and be prepared to alter your plans if unexpected expenses arise or if you learn of an activity or attraction that you hadn't initially considered. Excursions that are both memorable and reasonably priced may often be had by embracing the local culture and being open to new experiences.

Croatian budgeting demands careful planning, research, and adaptation. By organizing your costs, researching cost-effective options, and prioritizing your hobbies, you may maximize your holiday without going over your allotted spending limit. In Croatia, tourists may choose from a wide range of activities, from natural wonders to cultural delights, to fit every budget and interest.

Chapter 6: Tips for travelers

1. Visa Requirements: Verify Croatia's visa requirements before travelling. A considerable number of countries' citizens—including those from the United States, the European Union, and Canada—can enter Croatia without a visa for short trips.

The best times to visit Croatia are during the shoulder seasons of spring (April to June) and autumn (September to October), when the weather is pleasant and there are less visitors. July and August are the busiest and most costly months for travellers.

3. Money: The Croatian Kuna (HRK) is the accepted currency in this nation. Even though it's a good idea to carry some cash, most establishments accept credit cards.

4. Although English is widely used in tourist areas, Croatian is the official language. If you can pick up a few basic Croatian words, the locals could find it helpful and thankful.

5. Croatia's transportation infrastructure is highly linked. Buses connect large cities and towns and are the most widely used kind of public transportation. Although there are more trains, the network is still in its infancy. Ferries and catamarans are common ways to travel between islands.

6. Renting a car: If you want to go outside of major cities, renting a car is recommended. You have the freedom to visit remote areas and small towns. Verify the traffic laws in the area and confirm that you have an international driving permit.

7. Accommodation: There are many places to stay in Croatia, including hotels, guesthouses, apartments, and campers. It is recommended to

make bookings in advance during the busiest season.

8. Safety: Tourists generally feel secure traveling to Croatia. Nevertheless, it's wise to follow local advice and implement some basic safety precautions, such as keeping an eye on your belongings and avoiding isolated areas late at night.

9. The stunning national parks in Croatia are well known. Visit Plitvice Lakes National Park, Krka National Park, or Paklenica National Park to find hiking trails and awe-inspiring natural splendor.

10. Coastal spots: Croatia's coastline is home to a number of breathtaking spots. Don't miss Dubrovnik, Split, Zadar, and Hvar Island with its historical structures, charming old towns, and magnificent beaches.

11. Island hopping: Croatia is the ideal location for island hopping since it has more than a

thousand islands. Learn about the unique charm and pure waters of islands including Korula, Bra, Vis, and Mljet.

12. Regional Foods: Croatian cuisine has a pleasantly broad influence from Central European and Mediterranean cuisines. Consider sampling some of the local specialties, such as seafood, Pag cheese, Peka (slow-cooked meat and vegetables), and Croatian wines.

13. Although there is no official dress code in Croatia, it is advisable to dress modestly when entering places of worship. Bring comfortable, lightweight clothing, especially in the heat.

14. Sun Protection: It's crucial to apply sun protection because of Croatia's sunny Mediterranean climate. Drink plenty of water and put on sunscreen, a hat, and sunglasses.

15. Cultural etiquette: Respect local customs and traditions. When entering churches or monasteries, be respectful and well attired.

Learn a bit more about the cultural standards to avoid any unintended offense.

16. Explore the inner: While it's common knowledge that the coastline districts are beautiful, don't discount the equally stunning inner countryside. Visit Zagreb, Istria, Motovun and Rovinj, two charming hilltop towns, and the Plitvice Lakes.

17. Festivals & Events: Croatia hosts a lot of festivals every year. From traditional occasions like the Dubrovnik Summer Festival to modern music festivals like Ultra Europe and INmusic, there is always something happening.

18. Tap Water: Tap water is generally safe to drink in Croatia.

Frequently asked Questions

1. Where in Europe is Croatia?

A: Slovenia, Hungary, Serbia, Bosnia & Herzegovina, and Montenegro are the countries that border Croatia, which is situated in southeast Europe.

2. Where is Croatia's capital located?
A: Zagreb serves as Croatia's capital.

3. What is Croatia's official language?
A: Croatia's official language is Croatian.

4. What is the national currency of Croatia?

A: The Croatian Kuna (HRK) is the official currency of Croatia.

5. Do you know whether Croatia is a member of the EU?

A: Croatia joined the EU in 2013 and is now a member.

6. Do I need a visa to go to Croatia?

A: That depends on your country of origin. For a limited time, certain nationals of certain nations may need a visa to enter Croatia, while others may enter without one. For detailed visa requirements, check with the Croatian embassy or consulate in your nation.

7. When is Croatia at its most beautiful?

A: Between April and June and September and October, when the weather is beautiful and there are less tourists, are the ideal seasons to visit Croatia.

8. What are Croatia's most well-known tourist attractions?

A: The cities of Dubrovnik, Split, Zagreb, the Plitvice Lakes National Park, Hvar Island, and the Istrian Peninsula are among Croatia's most well-known tourist sites.

9. Is traveling to Croatia secure?

A: Travelers may feel secure visiting Croatia. However, like with any trip, it's crucial to use common sense, take the appropriate safety measures, and be aware of your surroundings.

10. Can I drink Croatian tap water?

A: In Croatia, drinking the tap water is typically safe.

11. How would you describe Croatian cuisine?

A variety of regional cuisines have influenced Croatian cooking. Some well-liked foods include sarma (stuffed cabbage rolls), cevapi (grilled minced pork), and numerous seafood dishes.

12. Is credit card use common in Croatia?

A: The majority of hotels, eateries, and stores in popular tourist locations accept credit cards. However, it's always a good idea to have extra cash on hand, particularly in more remote or smaller towns.

13. What voltage and plug types are used in Croatia?

A: The voltage in Croatia is 230V, and the plugs are either the Type C or Type F European standards.

14. A: Is it legal to use a cell phone in Croatia?

A local SIM card or an international roaming package from your carrier are also options for using an unlocked GSM phone in Croatia. For specifics and prices, check with your mobile service provider.

15. What are the top sights to visit in Dubrovnik?

A: The Old Town, Dubrovnik City Walls, Stradun (major street), Fort Lovrijenac, and the cable car to Mount Sr are some of the must-see sights in Dubrovnik.

16. Is Croatia home to any Game of Thrones shooting locations?

A: King's Landing in the television series Game of Thrones was mostly filmed in Dubrovnik.

17. Can I take a day excursion to the Plitvice Lakes National Park?

A: From Zagreb or other surrounding towns, you may travel by day to the Plitvice Lakes National Park. However, staying overnight in the region enables you to go further into the park.

18. Does Croatia have any sandy beaches?

A: Despite being recognized for its rugged coastline, Croatia also has several sandy beaches. Numerous locations, including Nin, Lopar (Rab Island), and Brela, have well-known sandy beaches.

19. Is renting a vehicle possible in Croatia?

A: In Croatia, you may hire a vehicle. At airports, cities, and tourist destinations, a variety of local and international automobile rental providers are accessible.

20. Is Croatian public transit simple to use?

A: It is easy to travel inside Croatia because to its well-developed public transportation infrastructure, which includes buses, trains, and ferries.

What conditions must be met before importing a pet into Croatia?

A pet passport or formal veterinarian certificate, evidence of rabies vaccination, and in rare situations, a microchip are required if you are bringing a pet to Croatia. Before visiting, it is a good idea to confirm the exact criteria with the Croatian government or your neighborhood embassy.

A: Yes, you may go to the Croatian islands.

A: Yes, Croatia has a large number of islands that are accessible by tourists. The most well-known ones are Hvar, Korula, Bra, Vis, and Pag.

23. How would you describe the climate in Croatia?

A: The climate in Croatia is varied, with the coastal regions having a Mediterranean climate with hot summers and moderate winters. The climate is more continental in inland areas, with hot summers and chilly winters.

24. Does Croatia have any national parks?

A: Yes, Croatia has a number of national parks, including Mljet, Krka, Paklenica, the Brijuni Islands, and the Plitvice Lakes. These parks include chances for hiking, swimming, and animal watching in addition to breathtaking natural beauty.

25. What is the exchange rate in Croatian currency?

A: The Croatian Kuna (HRK) and other currencies have varying exchange rates. Before traveling or converting money, it is advised to verify the exchange rates.

26. Is it possible to use euros in Croatia?

A: The Croatian Kuna is the country's official currency, despite the fact that it is a member of the EU. While some places in tourist regions could take euros, it is best to keep local cash on hand for smaller shops or rural locations.

27. Which water sports are the most popular in Croatia?

A: Water activities like kayaking, sailing, windsurfing, scuba diving, and snorkelling are all quite popular along Croatia's coastline.

Conclusion

Croatia is a beautiful, diverse country that offers visitors a wide range of experiences. From charming islands to charming ancient towns, Croatia has plenty to offer everyone. It also has magnificent coastal cities.

Consider visiting Croatia's best-known towns, like Dubrovnik, Split, and Zagreb, as well as the park's natural splendors and the nearby islands. Croatia may get crowded during the main vacation seasons, so research the best time to visit.

Enjoy Croatia's distinctive cuisine, which combines Central European and Mediterranean influences. Examine previous meals such as cevapi, sarma, and fresh seafood. Don't forget to sample some wine and olive oil as Croatia is known for producing both.

Using public transportation is straightforward in Croatia, and there are options for renting a car as well. Although visitors may tour the country without much concern, it's still a good idea to exercise caution and be mindful of your surroundings.

Before departing, confirm the visa requirements of your home country and confirm the validity of your passport. Despite the fact that English is widely spoken in tourist areas, it is nevertheless advisable to familiarize yourself with local customs and learn a few simple Croatian phrases.

Croatia offers a distinctive fusion of beautiful natural landscapes, extensive cultural heritage, and kind people. Whether it is in history, adventure, leisure, or gourmet delights, Croatia is a country that will mesmerize and leave lifelong memories.

Printed in Great Britain
by Amazon